Hawaiian Legends

Hawaiian Legends

William Hyde Rice

MINT EDITIONS

Hawaiian Legends was first published in 1923.

This edition published by Mint Editions 2023.

ISBN 9798888970072 | E-ISBN 9798888970225

Published by Mint Editions®

 MINT
EDITIONS

minteditionbooks.com

Publishing Director: Jennifer Newens
Design & Production: Rachel Lopez Metzger
Project Manager: Micaela Clark
Typesetting: Westchester Publishing Services

Contents

Preface

The collection of Hawaiian legends of which a translation is given in the following pages represents the work of many years by William Hyde Rice of Kauai. However, it is only within the last few years that Mr. Rice has translated the legends from his Hawaiian manuscripts. He has tried to make his version as literal as possible, preserving at the same time the spirit of the original Hawaiian, its flavor, rhythm, and phrasing. He has avoided adding modern embroidery of fancy, as well as figures of speech foreign to the Hawaiian language and to its mode of thought and expression.

For the furtherance of this aim, Mr. Rice has spent much of the past year in a complete review of his translation, adding and rejecting, and in every way attempting to approximate the spirit and letter of the Hawaiian.

Mr. Rice has been exceptionally well prepared for this work, as he has been familiar with the Hawaiian language from his earliest childhood. In fact until he was twenty, he never *thought* in English but always in Hawaiian, translating mentally into his mother tongue. In 1870 when he became a member of the House of Representatives, during the reign of Kamehameha V, Governor Paul Kanoa and S. M. Kamakau, the historian, both well-known Hawaiian scholars, gave Mr. Rice much help with his Hawaiian, especially teaching him the proper use of various complicated grammatical constructions, and explaining obscure variations in pronunciation and meaning.

The sources of the legends in this collection are varied. A number of the stories Mr. Rice remembers having heard as a child, and other rarer ones were gathered in later years. Many are from more than one source, but have corresponded even in details, and almost word for word. The legend of Kamapuaa, for instance, is one of the first which Mr. Rice remembers hearing. When a boy, the places mentioned in this story were pointed out to him: the spot where the demi-god landed, where he found the hidden spring, and where he rooted up the natives' sugar cane and sweet potatoes. The story of "The Small Wise Boy and the Little Fool" he has also been familiar with since childhood. The places mentioned in this tale can likewise be pointed out.

Most of the legends are from Kauai sources, but a number have been gathered from the other islands of the group. Whenever Mr. Rice heard of an old Hawaiian who knew any legends, he went to him, sometimes going to several to trace a special story, as for instance, the "Jonah and the Whale" story, "Makuakaumana," which after a long search he finally procured from Mr. Westervelt. This curious story seems to be more modern than the others of the collection. While hunting for a reliable Bernice P. Bishop Museum-Bulletin version of this story, Mr. Rice incidentally heard the story of "Manuwahi" at Heeia from an old Hawaiian.

"The Bird Man," "Holua-Manu," "The Destruction of Niihau's Akua," and "The Girl and the Mo-o," were obtained mainly from Mr. Francis Gay, who is one of the best living scholars of the Hawaiian language. The Niihau legend was heard from several other sources as well. Mr. Gay also gave the legends of the "Rainbow Princess" and the "Shrimp's Eyes": the ti plants mentioned in the latter legend can still be pointed out, growing at the mouth of a little valley near Holua-Manu. The Hawaiian manu script of part of the Menehune story was obtained from J. A. Akina, while the story of the "Rain Heiau" was told to him in 1912 by a man named Naialau, who has since died at Kalaupapa. "How Lizards Came to Molokai" and "Pakaa and Ku-a-pakaa" were told Mr. Rice by a man from Hawaii named Win, while the Rev. S. K. Kaulili, who is still living at Koloa, Kauai, gave him the most complete version of the "Rolling Island."

During Mr. George Carter's term as Governor, a reception was given in his honor, at Hanalei, where Mr. Rice was much interested in the very fine *oli* (chanting) of an old Hawaiian, named Kaululua. From him he obtained a number of legends, including that of "Ulukaa" and corresponding versions of others already in his collection. Other legends have been lost forever on account of ill-timed ridiculing by some chance companion, for Mr. Rice has found that the old people who know the legends are very sensitive, and when they find an unsympathetic auditor, refuse to continue their stories.

Mr. Rice's theory as to the origin of these legends is based on the fact that in the old days, before the discovery of the islands by Captain Cook, there were bards and storytellers, either itinerant or attached to the courts of the chiefs, similar to the minstrels and taletellers of medieval Europe. These men formed a distinct class, and lived only at the courts of the high chiefs. Accordingly, their stories were heard by none except those people attached to the service of the chiefs. This accounts for the loss of many legends, in later years, as they were not commonly known. These bards or storytellers sometimes used historical incidents or natural phenomena for the foundation of their stories, which were handed down from generation to generation. Other legends were simply fabrications of the imagination, in which the greatest "teller of tales" was awarded the highest place in the chief's favor. All these elements, fiction combined with fact, and shrouded in the mists of antiquity, came, by repetition, to be more or less believed as true.

This class of men were skillful in the art of the *apo*, that is, "catching" literally, or memorizing instantly at the first hearing. One man would recite or chant for two or three hours at a stretch, and when he had finished, his auditor would start at the beginning of the chant and go through the whole of the *mele* or story without missing or changing a word. These trained men received through their ears as we receive through our eyes, and in that way the ancient Hawaiians had a spoken literature, much as we have a written one. Mr. Rice has several times seen performances similar to the one described, where the two men were complete strangers to each other.

To the readers of this collection of Hawaiian legends the following biographical information will be of interest:

William Hyde Rice, the only son of William Harrison and Mary Hyde Rice, was born at Punahou, Honolulu, Hawaii, on July 23, 1846. At that time his parents, who had come to the islands as missionaries in 1840, were teachers at the school which had been established at Punahou in 1842 for the children of missionaries.

In 1854 the family moved to Lihue, Kauai, where the greater part of Mr. Rice's life has been spent. Besides his sisters his only young companions were Hawaiian boys, from whom as well as from his nurse, he readily learned the language. After a few years of teaching at home the boy was sent to Koloa, Kauai, to attend the boarding school of the Rev. Daniel Dole, whose son, Sanford Ballard Dole, was one of the boy's closest companions. Later, Mr. Rice attended Oahu College, Punahou, and Braton's College in Oakland, California.

Mr. Rice served in the House of Representatives from 1870 to 1872 (the year of his marriage to Miss Mary Waterhouse in Honolulu), 1873, 1882, 1887, 1889, and 1890, and as a member of the Senate from 1895 to 1898. He was one of the thirteen committeemen who waited upon King Kalākaua, giving him twenty-four hours to sign the constitution. and was Governor of Kauai under Queen Liliuokalani until after the revolution in 1893.

In the present translation Mr. Rice has received much able and sympathetic assistance from Miss Katherine McIntyre in a secretarial capacity, extending over a period of several years. Miss Ethel Damon has been of inestimable value in her sound judgments and encouragement, and it has been my privilege to assist my grandfather during the past year. No one who has only read these legends can fully appreciate the charm of them as told by Mr. Rice in person. Many of them he still recites word for word in Hawaiian. One of the most vivid memories of my childhood will always be that of hearing my grandfather tell these legends, as he pointed out to us the places mentioned in the stories.

Lihue, January, 1923
Edith J.K. Rice

The Goddess Pele

P ele was the daughter of Moemo and Haumea, both well-known names in the oldest Hawaiian legends. Many other children were born to this couple, seven illustrious sons and six distinguished daughters. The youngest sister of Pele, Hiiaka-ika-poli-o-Pele, was born into the world as an egg. Pele concealed this egg under her arm until the child was hatched, and ever afterwards showed great affection for her.

When Pele had grown to womanhood, she begged her parents' consent to travel. This was granted, and wrapping Hiiaka in her pa-u, or tapa skirt, the adventurous Pele set forth.

She traveled first to the kingdom of her brother, Kamohoalii, Champion of the King. When he inquired where she was going Pele replied, "I shall first find Pola-pola. From there I shall go to the land of Kauihelani, where Kane hides the islands. I shall then find the far-reaching lands, the kingdom of Kacahi, the Fire-Thrower-Niihau."

To help his sister in this long journey Kamohoalii gave her the canoe of their brother, the Whirlwind, Pu-ahiohio, and his paddlers, the Tide, Keaulawe, and the Currents, Keau-ka. Stepping into this canoe Pele was snatched away at once by the wind. Kamohoalii looked after her and called, "Go your way. I shall soon follow with your relations."

In a short time Pele, borne by the magic canoe, reached Niihau. She ordered the canoe to return to her brother as she hoped the queen would give her another one. Then, crossing the salt marshes, she came at evening to the dwelling of the queen, Kaoahi, whose guards cried out that a beautiful stranger was coming. When Pele was brought before Kaoahi her beauty astonished the queen, who had never before seen a woman whose back was as straight as a *pali*[1] and whose breasts were rounded like the moon.

Great aloha grew in the heart of the queen for her guest, and before eating together they took the oath of friendship. Then they retired to the beds made of fine Niihau mats where they slept until the cocks crowed.

Early in the morning the queen sent forth her messengers to summon the *konohiki*, the overseers of the land, who were ordered to instruct all

---

1. See glossary for Hawaiian words not defined in text.

the people of the island to bring presents for Kaoabi's great friend. Each person brought his gift to Pele without a word of complaining.

Every day for ten days Pele entered into the games, the hula dancing, the surfboard riding, and the other pleasures of the people. Everyone was eager to talk with the beautiful stranger, and Pele saw all that was in their minds.

One day the beautiful guest disappeared. The queen thought she had gone to visit one of the chiefs. No amount of search could reveal her hiding place. The *kahuna* were called together to divine where the woman had gone. At last they said to Kaoahi, "O Queen! The Night tells us that Pele is not a human being like you. She is an *akua*. She has many bodies."

These words aroused great wonder on Niihau as to how Pele had come and where she had gone.

After her sudden disappearance Pele went to Point Papaa from where she looked across to Kauai. Taking on her spirit body, she quickly passed through Mana and the mountains back of Waimea and came to Haena.

As darkness fell she heard the hula drums beating. Following the call of the music Pele came to a rude enclosure where the people were gathered for sports. In the crowd she saw a very handsome man, Lohiau, the king of Kauai, whom she suddenly resolved to seek for her husband.

The assembly was startled by hearing a beautiful voice chanting a *mele* of the hills, and by seeing at the door a woman of wondrous beauty and charm.

Lohiau ordered the people to stand aside so that the stranger could enter. The chiefs of Kauai crowded around Pele, wondering who she was. Lohiau was surprised when his unknown guest asked him to become her husband. He did not consent until he heard that she was Pele, the mortal.

Then Lohiau bade his servants prepare the tables for a feast, and he invited Pele to sit with him and partake of the food. After the meal was eaten Pele told Lohiau that she could not live with him until she had found a suitable home for them. The king of Kauai was rather ashamed to have his wife prepare the home, but he consented.

Kaleiapaoa, Lohiau's best and truest friend, was summoned to see Pele. But before he looked upon her he hurried to the king's sister, the celebrated tapa maker of Kalalau, and asked for a pa-u. She gave him one she had just made by beating with *lauae* from the cliffs of Honopu. Pele was very much pleased with this pa-u because it was so sweet scented. When she had finished admiring it, she said to Lohiau, "Now I shall go to prepare our house."

At once she began to dig a cave, but striking water she left it. She tried again and, meeting with the same results, left Haena and came to the *kukui* grove near Pilaa. Pleased with this spot she turned to the mountains where she dug as before, but met with unsatisfactory results.

Taking the form of an old woman, Pele hurried to Koloa. There she again struck water. Repeated efforts to dig a dry cave having failed, she decided to leave Kauai and to find on Oahu a suitable place for her home.

Pele landed at Kaena on Oahu. Near the hill Kapolei she again began to search for a home. As before she soon struck water. Discouragement filled her heart and looking toward Kauai she wept for her loved one there.

Walking through the wiliwili trees Pele reached Kuwalaka-i where she took her egg-like sister, Hiiaka, from her pa-n and placing her safely on the ground hurried to the sea for *limu*, or seaweed, from which she squeezed the juice for drinking water.

Pele decided to spend the night in this place. She called the flowers which grew there "the pa-u of Hiiaka" and she crowned her fair head with a lei of them. As she slept, her lover appeared before her. This vision brought courage to Pele and early in the morning she hurried on her way.

On the heights of Moanalua, near Honolulu, Pele tried again to dig a dry cave. Striking salt water, she called the place Alia-paakai, the Salt-Marsh. When she came to Makapuu she saw the chiefess Malei, the Wreath, stringing flowers for a lei, while her subjects were cleaning the fish they had just brought from the sea.

At the little harbor of Hanauma a canoe was being prepared for a trip to Molokai. There Pele shook off her spirit body and as a beautiful woman greeted the men. At the sight of her great beauty they all fainted. When they had recovered, Pele asked them to take her to Molokai with them. They readily consented.

When Pele jumped ashore on Molokai, she became invisible and disappeared. The captain of the crew told the king about the beautiful woman who had come with him from Oahu. The whole island was searched, but Pele could not be found.

In the meantime Pele had dug a cave between Kalaupapa and Kalawao. Finding water, she left Molokai and hurried to Maui. She traveled over Maui from end to end hunting for a suitable place for her home. Finding none, she was greatly grieved and filled the whole island with Pele's smoke, and then hastened on to Hawaii.

Pele landed at Puna on Hawaii. She decided to call first on the god of the island, Ailaau, the Wood-Eater, who had his dwelling at Kilauea. When Ailaau saw Pele coming towards his home, he disappeared because he was afraid of her.

Pele began to dig. At last success crowned her efforts. Digging day and night, she came to fire and knew that this spot would be suitable for the long-sought home. She decided to make a home large enough for all her many brothers and sisters.

After the fiery pit was dug. Pele changed her egg-like sister, Haka, into human form and the two lived happily in her new home.

One day Hiiaka went down to the forest of Panaewa near Hilo. There she saw a girl so skilled in making leis of lehua blossoms that she longed to make of her a personal friend. Hiiaka learned that her name was Hopoe, and she spoke to her in these words, "Now that we are friends you must go wherever I go. Wherever I sleep you shall sleep. We shall never be parted."

Hopoe was very happy and answered, "I spend my time making leis. I have planted two groves of trees, one white and one red. These I give to you."

So Hiiaka returned to Kilauea with her friend who pleased Pele very much by teaching her to make leis of lehua flowers. Soon all Pele's household was busily stringing the flowers.

As Pele worked she heard the voice of her beloved Lohiau calling her, for the wind carried his sad song to her ears. So Pele called her sisters to her and asked each one to go to Kauai to find her husband. All refused. Then Pele commanded Hiiaka, "Go to Kauai and bring my husband to me. Do not dare to kiss him, lest some dire disaster befall you. Be gone no longer than forty days." All agreed that it was wise for Hiiaka to go, as she was the youngest.

Stretching out her right hand to her sister, Pele bestowed upon her all the supernatural powers she possessed, so that the journey could be accomplished in safety.

Hiiaka prepared for the journey and as she worked she sang a *mele* in which she voiced her complaint that she should go alone to Haena for the handsome Lohiau. Pele heard her and cheered her by saying that she would meet someone who would go with her.

So with a sad heart Hiiaka set forth on her sister's errand. Looking back she saw her home in the volcano where her brothers and sisters were sitting like stone images. She called to them to care for her beloved grove of lehua trees.

As she entered the forest above Hilo she met Wahine-omao, the Steadfast-Woman, who was on her way to carry gifts of pig and sugar cane as a sacrifice to Pele. Thinking that Hiiaka was Pele, Wahine-omao laid her gifts before her. Hiiaka saw that the stranger was mistaken and spoke these words to her: "I am not Pele. She is still in Kilauea. Carry your presents there. After you have reached Kilanea descend into Halemaumau where you will see many beautiful women bedecked with lehua leis. Sacrifice your gifts to an old woman lying on a pillow made of wiliwili wood and covered with Puna mats, for she is Pele."

Wahine-omao, still believing that Pele stood before her, replied, "Do not deal falsely with me. No doubt you are Pele. I shall give you my gifts and so spare myself the long journey."

Finally Hiiaka made it clear that she was not Pele, and the woman departed with her gifts. With the aid of her supernatural powers Hiiaka put such speed into her feet that she traveled as fast as the whirlwind, and in no time came to Halemaumau and gave her gifts to the old woman. At once old age left Pele and she became the most beautiful of all in the pit.

Then Pele asked the stranger, "Did you meet a woman as you came? Go back and meet her again. Become friendly with her and travel with her."

Wahine-omao did as she was told and soon overtook Hiiaka whom she told what Pele had commanded. Looking back the lonely Hiiaka saw the smoke rising from the home of Pele. She saw her sisters and friends going to the sea. She saw her beloved grove of lehua trees being destroyed by a lava flow. Bitterness filled her heart and she wept over her fate.

Wahine-omao, who could not see what her companion saw, upbraided her with these words, "How do you know these things? We are in the forest and cannot see beyond its limits. Complain no more, for you weary me."

So in silence they walked on until they came to Hilo where the king was having games. In the midst of the people two beautiful women decorated with leis of seafoam were singing. As the eyes of the king fell upon Hiiaka and her companion, he was startled to see how far their beauty surpassed the beauty of the singers.

When Hiiaka saw the beautiful women she said, "These are not women. They are *akua*."

The king replied, "*Akua* would not come at midday and eat and drink with us. These women refused to sing until we had given them presents."

Hiiaka still contended that they were not what they appeared to be and asked the king, "Allow me to try them. If I look at them and they depart you will know that they are *akua*. If they stay you will know that they are human."

To this request the king replied, "What wager will you place that they are not human?"

Hiiaka answered, "My companion and I have no property, but we will wager our bodies"

Whereupon a man in the crowd called, "It is not good to wager one's body. Let me back your wager with my property."

To the king's question as to what his property consisted of he replied that he owned a canoe, a fishing net, a patch of sugar cane, several taro patches and a pig. Against all these things the king wagered two storehouses filled with food and tapa and the land on which these buildings stood.

As soon as these wagers had been placed, Hiiaka approached the women. When they saw her, one said, "She is our lord." Whereupon they ran. Hiiaka followed and put them both to death as her supernatural powers were greater than theirs.

As she returned to the king the crowd cheered her for her beauty and bravery. The king paid his wager and Hiiaka gave it to the man who had helped her. Calling Wahine-omao, Hiiaka hurried on to the river Wailuku, where they saw a man ferrying freight. He agreed to take them across the river, and so the friends left Hilo and entered the forest, where their path was beset by akua trying to delay them. Hiiaka killed all who blocked their way and came at last to the plains of Makiki.

By this time the forty days allotted for making the journey to Kauai had expired, but Hiiaka decided to go on anyway. More troubles befell them. A certain king, Maka'ukiu, tried to block their way by causing huge waves to break over the cliffs so that they could not swim around the point. Hiiaka prayed and the sea became calm.

So they traveled on. A bird flew over them carrying a spray of begonia in its bill. Hiiaka sang a *mele* in which she expressed a wish for a safe journey on the errand of her powerful sister Pele.

Finally they came upon some men loading a canoe with gifts which they said were to be taken to Olepau, the king of Maui. The women asked to be taken in the canoe. The men consented and the next morning they reached Kahikinui on Maui.

As soon as the canoe grated on the beach, the two young women sprang ashore and called to the canoe-men that they were going to search for a bath. In fact they hurried on to Keala where the plains had been burned off. There the natives were catching plover with baited sticks. Hiiaka startled them with these words, "I am sorry for the king of Maui. He is dead. You are so engrossed in catching plover and grasshoppers that you have no time for your king."

The people could not believe these words, but nevertheless, they returned home and found that they were indeed true. Their king was dead. They hurried to the celebrated prophet and told him that two young women had made known to them the king's death. When he had heard the description of the women, the prophet said that they were Hiiaka and Wahine-omao. He sent messengers as swift as arrows shot from the bow to overtake them.

When Hiiaka saw these messengers following her she changed herself and her companion into feeble old women. Soon the messengers overtook them and asked if they had seen anything of two beautiful young women.

Hiiaka answered that two such women had passed them long before. The messengers hurried on but, overtaking no one, they returned to the prophet and told him their experience.

The prophet knew that the old women were Hiiaka and Wahine-oman in disguise. He said that they must be brought back before the king could come to life. This time he did not trust their capture to messengers, but he himself swam around the point and met them coming from the other direction.

Hiiaka consented to return and restore the king to life. She told the prophet to go ahead and gather all the sweet smelling herbs. This he did in the twinkling of an eye, but Hiiaka and her friend had reached the king and brought him to life before the prophet got there. Then the prophet knew that the women were *akua*.

Inquiring whither they were bound he learned that they were on their way to Haena to find Lohiau. The prophet ordered the king's canoe-men to bring out the canoe and to take the travelers to Koolau on Oahu.

After an uneventful trip of a day and a night the friends were landed at Koolau. The canoe-men asked them where they were going and were told that Ewa was their destination. The men answered that Ewa was *kapu* for them, so they rested near the sea.

Then Hiiaka began her journey to the Nuuanu Pali. The woman in charge of the Pali tried to delay her, but was struck down by the prowess of the stranger.

After this there were no difficulties encountered as they made their way to Kalihi. There they saw a great many people diving for clams. Nearby two men were preparing a canoe for a trip to Kauai, Hiiaka told them that she had heard many times of Kauai but had no way of going there. The men, noticing that the speaker and her friend were young and beautiful, generously offered them a seat in their canoe.

As the sea was rough Hiiaka wanted to help with the paddling, but the men were strong and never became tired. They landed at Wailua and encountered many difficulties in traveling from there to Haena.

First a certain *kupua*, the demi-god of the locality, guarding the surf, saw them coming and sent messengers to see if they walked over the ti leaf without breaking it, which was a sign that they were supernatural beings—*akua*. Hiiaka deceived them by sending Wahine-omao ahead as she was more human and her feet tore the leaves. The messengers returned and reported that the strangers were human beings.

Next they came upon a *kupua* swollen to twice his natural size, but he was unable to stop them.

Near Kealia they came upon a man cooking his *luau* or young taro leaves to eat with his poi. Hiiaka by her magic power, cooked the *luau* in a few minutes.

Looking into the man's house Hiiaka saw a very sick woman whom all the *kahuna* had been unable to help. Hiiaka uttered a prayer and at once health was given back to the woman.

Having done this act of kindness, Hiiaka went on her way to Hanalei. At the valley of Kiaiakua, the *akua* were lying in wait to stop them. As one tried to block their way, Hiiaka gave him a blow like a stroke of lightning and he fell back stunned.

At the mouth of the Hanalei River, they again met resistance from an angry *akua*, who was struck to earth as the others had been.

Coming to Kealahula, they saw Hoohila combing her hair. She, too, tried to delay their journey by making the sea break over the cliff.

Wahine-omao threw sand into the eyes of the *akua*, and this difficult was overcome.

Near Wainiha they were treated more kindly. The great fisherman of the place killed his favorite dog for them and then gave games in their honors.

So the travelers were nearing their journey's end. As they came to the wet caves dug by Pele in her efforts to find a suitable home for herself and Lohiau, Kilioe, the sister of Lohiau, saw them, covered with lehua leis, and knew that they had come for her brother. Kilioe was the great hula dancer and teacher. No one could hula in public on Kauai unless approved by her and given the *uniki*, the sign which served in place of a diploma.

But, alas, the beloved Lohiau was dead and in a *mele* Kilioe made known this sad fact to Hiiaka. Hiiaka was not discouraged, for magic power was in her hands and she set about overcoming this difficult, apparently the greatest of all.

As luck would have it, she saw the spirit of Lohiau flying over one of the points nearby. He was beckoning to her. Hiiaka gave to Wahine-omao swiftness of flight and together they chased the elusive spirit over many a sleep *pali*. When they came to the ladder of Nualolo, the weary Wahine-omao cried, "Indeed you must love this Lohiau greatly."

At last Hiiaka caught the spirit in a flower and hurried back to the *pali* above the wet caves where the body of Lohiau had been laid. Then she began her task of putting the spirit back into the body.

Kaleipaoa was fishing and grieving over the death of his truest friend. Looking towards the mountains he was startled to see a fire. At first he thought it was only the spirit of Lohiau, but as it continued to burn he thought that someone must be attempting to steal the body of his chief. Quickly coming ashore, he silently climbed up the *pali* and was greatly surprised to see two beautiful women trying to put the spirit back into Lohiau's body. This sight filled him with gladness and he returned to his home, where he told his wife what was being done by strangers.

In the meantime, Hiiaka was patiently accompling her task. She put the spirit back into the body through an incision in the great toe, but she found it very difficult to get the spirit past the ankles and the knee joints. However, after she had worked for eight days, Lohiau was restored to life. Hiiaka carried him to his home and bathed him in the sea on five successive nights, as was the custom. At the end of that time he was purified, so that he could again mingle with his friends.

Then for the first time in many days Hiiaka and Wahine-omao slept very soundly. Lohiau's sister passed by the house and, seeing the door open, entered. She was surprised to see her brother sleeping soundly. She beat the drum and made known to all the people that Lohiau, their chief, was alive again. Many came, bringing gifts with grateful hearts.

Hiiaka was very anxious to start for Hawaii, as the forty days allotted her had long since expired and she feared that Pele would be angry.

At Kealia the chief entertained the three guests with sports in which Lohiau was very skillful. Reaching Kapaa, they met the king, who gave them a canoe to carry them to Oahu.

After a short stay on this island, where there was much dancing and royal feasting, the travelers left for Hawaii. As they were passing Molokai, Hiiaka saw a chiefess standing near the shore and asked her to give them fish. The chiefess replied, "I have no fish for you, proud slave." These words so angered Hiiaka that she swam ashore and killed her.

After this adventure they went on quietly until they reached Hawaii, where they landed at Puna and then hastened on towards the home of Pele and to a relentless fate.

When they came to the brink of the volcano, Hiiaka sent Wahine-omao ahead to greet Pele while she and Lohiau stayed behind. There in full view of Pele and her sisters, Hiiaka, suddenly overcome with emotion for the man she had grown to love, threw her arms around him and kissed him.

Pele's anger knew no bounds. She cried, "Why did she not kiss Lohina while they were on Kauai? She does it before my eyes to laugh at me."

Seeking revenge, Pele sent her sisters to destroy her lover by means of a lava flow. They put on their fire robes and went forth rather unwillingly. When they came near and saw how handsome Lohiau was, pity took hold of them and they cast only a few cinders at his feet and returned to Pele in fear. Hiiaka knew that the falling cinders would be followed by fire, so she told Lohiau to pray.

When Pele saw her people returning from their unaccomplished errand she sent them back, commanding them to put aside their pity for the handsome man. So the fire burst forth again and gradually surrounded Lohiau. At last the rocky lava covered his body.

When Hiiaka saw what her sister had done, she was so angry that she dug a tunnel from the volcano to the sea, through which she poured the fire, leaving only a little in the crater. This small amount was kept by one of her brothers under his arm.

WILLIAM HYDE RICE

Seeing what Hiiaka was doing, Pele became alarmed and sent Wahine-omao to beg her to spare her sisters. Hiiaka did not heed her friend and Pele cried, "This is a punishment sent upon me because I did not care for Hiiaka's friend, and I allowed her lehua trees to be burned."

Wahine-omao again entreated Hiiaka to spare Pele, recalling to her mind the many days of travel they had spent together. At last Hiiaka promised to spare Pele but refused to see her again.

As soon as possible she returned to Kauai and told the faithful Kaleia-paoa what Pele had done. This true friend of Lohiau made a solemn vow to pull out the eyelashes of Pele and to fill her mouth with dirt.

Led by the magic power of Hiiaka, Kaleiapaoa soon reached the outer brink of the crater and began to attack Pele with vile names. Pele answered by urging him to come down and carry out his oath. Attempting many times to descend and punish Pele, he was always forced back. At last Pele allowed him to come before her, but he no longer wished to carry out his threat. Pele had conquered him by her beauty and charm. After he had remained in the crater four days, he was persuaded to return to Kauai with Hiiaka as his wife.

Two brothers of Pele who had come from foreign lands, saw Lohiau's body lying as a stone where the lava flow had overtaken him. Pity welled up in their hearts and they brought Lohiau to life again. One of these brothers made his own body into a canoe and carried the unfortunate Lohian to Kauai, where he was put ashore at Ahukini.

Coming to Hanamaulu, Lohiau found all the houses but one closed. In that one were two old men, one of whom recognized him and asked him to enter. The men were making tapa which they expected to carry soon to Kapaa, where games were being held in honor of Kaleiapaoa and his bride, Hiiaka.

As soon as the tapa was prepared, the men, joined by Lohiau, started for the sports. At the Wailua River discussion arose. Lohiau wanted to swim across, but the men insisted on carrying him over on the palms of their outstretched hands.

When they reached Waipouli, Lohiau suggested that the men carry the tapa over a stick, so that he could be concealed between its folds. This was done and at last they came close to Hiiaka.

Lohiau told the men to enter the *kilu* game. Lohiau promised to *oli* for them in case they were struck. First the old man was struck, and from his hiding place Lohiau sang a song that he and Hiiaka had sung in their travels. The next night in the game the other old man was struck, and Lohiau sang the song that he and Hiiaka had composed as they neared the volcano.

Hiiaka knew that these were the songs that she and Lohiau had sung together during their days of travel. She lifted up the tapa and saw again Lohiau—the man twice restored to life from death, the lover for whom she had dared the wrath of Pele, the mate whom she now encircled with loving arms.

When Kaleiapaoa saw that his old friend had returned, his shame and sorrow were so great that he hastened to the sea and threw himself into the water to meet his death.

So, at last, Hiiaka and Lohiau were united—and lived happily at Haena for many years.

The Rainbow Princess

A Legend Of Kauai

A FAMILY OF HAWAIIANS WERE moving into the valley of Nualolo, on the Napali coast. To reach this valley it was necessary to climb up a swinging ladder, which hung over the cliff. One man was carrying a baby girl, and as he swung on to the swaying ladder he dropped the child. The parents, in agony, watched their baby falling but were overjoyed to see the *akua* of the rainbow catch her up before she struck the water, and carry her on the rainbow over the mountains down to Waimea valley. In this valley, they placed her in a small cave beneath a waterfall. There she lived, watched over by the *akua*, who always sent the rainbow to care for her. There she grew, at length, into beautiful womanhood, and everyday she sat in the sunshine on the rocks above the cave with a rainbow above her head.

Then it happened that a prince from Waimea fell deeply in love with the beautiful Rainbow princess, as she was called. He would hasten to the rocks above the waterfall and try to woo her. But his efforts were all in vain, for with a merry laugh she would dive into the water and call to him, "When you can call me by name, I will come to you."

At last, growing sick with longing for the princess, he journeyed to Maui and Hawaii to consult the *kahuna* in regard to the girl's name. Alas, none could help him!

In despair he returned to Waimea and called on his old grandmother who inquired the reason for his great sadness. The prince replied, "I love the Rainbow Princess who lives in the waterfall. She only laughs at me and tells me that when I can call her by name she will be my wife. I have consulted all the *kahuna* and none can tell me her name."

With these words the grandmother cheered the heart of the sorrowing prince, "If you had come to me I could have told you her name. Go to the waterfall. When the princess laughs at you, call her U-a, which means rain."

The prince hastened to the waterfall and when he called "U-a" the beautiful maiden went to him. They were married and lived together many happy years.

Ulukaa, The Rolling Island

Kaeweaoho, the king of Waipio, Hawaii, was greatly beloved by his people because he gave them a beneficent government. After he had reigned a short time he chose two men from his people as his personal fishermen. Fishing was one of his favorite sports. He often asked his fishermen to allow him to go fishing with them, but they always refused to take him because they feared some accident might befall them at sea, and their king would be in danger.

The king showed such favoritism to his fishermen that his head steward became very jealous and in his heart plotted injury to them. One day when the men were away fishing the head steward left no food at their homes. When the fishermen returned from the king's fishing with baskets full of fish they found no food at their homes. Being very hungry they kept a few of the smaller fish from the king's basket.

The next morning they went fishing as usual. They returned at night and again found no food at their homes. This time they believed that the king had given his order that no food be left for them. They could not understand the king's neglect, for they had always served him faithfully and had brought to him their entire catch of fish. Anger against their lord grew in their hearts and they decided to get revenge in this manner: The next time the king asked to go fishing with them, they would take him and would leave him in the deep sea. They prepared their canoe. They placed in it four paddles and two gourd bailers. Under their fishing tackle they concealed two paddles and one gourd.

Early the next morning the young king, Kaeweaoho, came to his fishermen and begged them to take him with them as the sea was very smooth. They answered, "Yes, O King, today you shall go with us for the sea is smooth and we have too often refused your request."

They got into the canoe and paddled out until the sea hid the land.

The king often asked, "Where are your fishing grounds?"

To this question the fishermen replied, "See the white caps yonder. There we shall find the best fishing. Where the sea drinks in the point of Hanakaki, there lies Hina's canoe. There we shall drop anchor."

The king thought that fish were to be found nearer land, but they told him that only *poopaa*, the easiest fish to catch, were in the shallow water. In the deep sea all the best fish lived.

When land could no longer be seen, the two fishermen began to carry out their cruel plan. One man dropped his paddle, saying that a wave had knocked it from his hand. Then the gourd and the other paddle were dropped into the sea and were carried away by the waves.

The king, seeing the danger they were in, said, "I am the young man here. Let me swim for the paddles, which are still close by. The we can go safely home."

One of the men replied, "Do not jump into the sea. The big fish will devour you." But the king heeded not and was soon swimming for the paddles. Then the fishermen took out their hidden paddles and turned the canoe towards land.

The bewildered king called to them, "Come and save your king I have done wrong I shall right it. You shall have lands. Come and get me or I shall die."

The fishermen paddled away as fast as they could. Then the king looked about him and saw no signs of land. He wept bitterly, fearing that he would never again see his parents. While the unhappy king was weeping in great distress, the rainbow, the fine mist, and the red glow, signs that he was a high chief, hung over him.

As Kaeweaoho was swimming, Kuwahailo, Kaanaelike's grandfather, looked down from the sky and seeing the high chief signs hovering over a swimmer knew that the man must be a very high chief or a king who would make a suitable husband for his favorite granddaughter, who lived on Ulukaa. So he decided to save the swimmer.

At once a great storm arose on the sea, and Kuwahailo moved the rolling island close to the young king. Kaeweaoho was alarmed when he heard the big waves breaking on the land. He thought it was the big fish coming to devour him. Just as his strength was failing a breaker rolled him upon the soft sand where he lay as one dead.

When life returned to him he was greatly surprised to find himself on land. He tried to rise but was scarcely able to do so, as his limbs were cramped from the many hours he had spent in the water. He fell back on the warm sand and slept for many hours. At last the heat of the sun awakened him. He stood up and saw that the land was very beautiful. As he was looking about hunger whispered to him, "Do not tarry to admire the landscape. Walk on until you find something to eat." The king did as hunger bade him and finding ripe bananas ate of them, and strength returned to him.

After Kaeweaoho had eaten he decided to go on to see if he could find who inhabited this beautiful land. He had not gone far before he came upon a large taro patch, the banks of which were covered with breadfruit, sweet potatoes, sugar cane, and bananas. The king eagerly partook of food and his beauty returned like the beauty of the young banana leaf.

Kaeweacho saw no signs of any house. He wondered to whom such a beautiful island belonged. While he was wondering, the queen of the island, Kaanaelike, was watching him secretly, admiring his beauty and rejoicing over the coming of such a handsome creature. She had never seen a man before. At last her curiosity led her to speak thus to the stranger: "I grieve to see you eating food which is poisonous, food which only birds should eat. We of this land eat only berries." These words carried to Kaeweaoho the knowledge that all these fruits had not been planted by the hand of man.

When the queen asked the stranger whence he had come, he answered, "I have long heard of the beauties of this land. Now I hear the music of your voice. If I speak in the language of my land you will ridicule I came from the sea where a cruel wave wrecked my canoe. Give me food, for I am hungry."

Kaanaelike led the way to her house from which she brought out berries for the king to eat. The king told her that he could not eat raw food, and asked her why she did not cook the fruit. The queen replied that cooking was unknown to her and also to her parents, who were in the mountains gathering berries.

Kaeweaoho saw many dead trees nearby so he gathered the dry boughs and after having made an *imu* he rubbed two dry sticks together as he had seen his servants do in his far away island. He found it difficult to get a spark of fire but at last he was successful. He then bent over the tiny fame to strengthen it by blowing in it. Suddenly it blazed up and burnt off his eyebrows. The first fire of the king was not a very successful one, but he made another which proved to be a good one. After the king had placed the food in the *imu* to cook, he went to fish. When he had caught a few fish he came back and lying down beside the *imu*, fell asleep.

The queen found him there and believing him dead, cried, "Why did you labor so hard! You have killed yourself, my beautiful one."

These words awakened the king, who hurriedly uncovered his *imu*. He took out the taro and after peeling it ate the first food he had ever cooked. Busy thoughts filled his mind, thoughts of how changed his life was. As a king he had been born to every luxury. Now he was an outcast working to find food to keep his body alive.

WILLIAM HYDE RICE

Soon he put aside these sad thoughts and called to Kaanaelike to come and taste the cooked food. She feared it would poison her and that she would never see her parents again, but the king told her it would make her grow more beautiful. At last he persuaded her to try first the taro, then the breadfruit. After a time Kaanaelike tasted the sweet potato, which the king said would give her great strength and beauty. She was surprised to find that no harm came to her.

Kaanaelike asked the Man-from-the-Sea, as she called the king, to go home with her. When he reached her house he found it filled with berries. These the queen threw out, and making a bed of mats, gave the stranger a room. Thus they lived for two months. Daily he cooked food and fish in his *imu* and the queen eating thereof grew more beautiful.

At the end of two months Kaanaelike's parents sent messengers from the mountains with packs loaded with berries. As they neared the house they saw their queen eating the cooked food, so dropping their packs they rushed back to the mountains crying, "The queen will be killed! The queen will be killed!"

As soon as the queen's parents heard these words they ordered everyone to follow them to the seashore.

When Kaanaelike saw the messengers running back to the mountains she spoke to Kaeweaoho in this manner: "Man-from-the-Sea, dig a hole under my room. We will line it with mats and there you can hide so that my parents will not kill you when they come." This they did and she hid the king.

When her parents came Kaanaelike ate the cooked food. At once they and their followers began to wail, thinking that she would die. She told her parents that she would not die. She had eaten of this food for two months, and they could see that she was more beautiful and stronger than before. She persuaded them to eat of the cooked food and she gave the remainder to the followers.

Then her parents asked Kaanaelike how she had learned to cook food. She told them that the Man-from-the-Sea, who had been very kind to her, had taught her. Her parents said, "If these things you tell us are true the Man-from-the-Sea must be very good."

No longer fearing for his life, Kaanaelike removed the mats and led forth the king, whom she said she loved and wished to marry. Her parents told her that this could not be without the consent of her grandfather. Kaanaelike asked where her grandfather lived, and learned that his home was in the sky.

In order to visit her grandfather to gain his consent, Kaanaelike was directed to a large calabash which concealed a small coconut tree. This tree she was told to climb. Before she began to climb it her parents gave her the sacred pa-u, or skirt, which she was to hold on her lap and no harm would ever befall her.

No sooner had the queen climbed into the tree than it began to grow. It and grew until it reached the deep blue of heaven. In the sky she found an opening which led into the kingdom of her grandfather. She went in, and as soon as she had left the tree it grew smaller and smaller. until it reached its original size.

After watching the coconut tree disappear Kaanaelike saw a path which she followed until she came to two guards keeping watch over a large stone hollowed out like a huge pot. The guards urged this woman to depart at once before their master came, for he spared neither man, woman, nor child; all shared the same cruel death in the pot.

Kaanaelike did not obey them but asked for her grandfather, Kuwahailo. The guards replied, "You are asking for our lord. He has gone to hunt for more victims to fill his pot. He takes any person he finds, old or young, until his pot is full. He heats a huge stone until it is red hot, then he rolls it into the pot, and so cooks his victims. You see all about you the bones of many victims. Therefore, be advised, you who are young and beautiful. If you wish to live return at once by the path you came."

But Kaanaelike was determined to see her grandfather and asked which way he had gone. The guards said that he had gone to the East looking for victims to hurl into his pot. Then the granddaughter asked where their lord slept and they answered, "It is not known to us. His home is held sacred. It is *kapu* for us, his servants, to go there. We have warned you. Now depart if you wish to live."

Still Kaanaelike questioned them: "When does your mighty lord return?"

To this they answered that she would know, for the land would quake, the trees would be bent over, and the wind would blow. First his tongue would come with victims in its hollow. Then his body would follow.

After Kaanaelike had heard all these things she followed a path which led to a cave. In the cave was a pile of bones of chiefs whom the king had eaten. Nearby was a smooth stone used as a pillow by the king. The queen was becoming very weary and so she rolled up her sacred pa-u, and using it as a pillow, lay down on the mats to rest. Suddenly she

WILLIAM HYDE RICE

felt the earthquake and heard the wind blowing. Then she remembered that these were the signs of the coming of her grandfather.

When Kuwahailo reached his guards he called out in a loud voice, "I smell the blood of a mortal!"

In fear the guards answered, "We have seen no one pass by. Someone may have passed behind us. We saw no one as we were busy guarding the pot."

The angry king said, "If you lie to me I shall eat you both!" Then he looked to the cast, and west, and south. He saw no one. As he turned towards his home, he cried, "The presumptuous mortal has dared to enter my cave. He will answer for this by his death!"

Before entering his home the king unfastened his huge tongue and hung it at the side of the cave. As soon as he stepped into the cave he saw a woman lying on his bed. Violent anger possessed him. He tried to seize her, but when he touched her he received a severe shock, almost like a kick. The sacred pa-n was protecting Kaanaelike. Kuwahailo knew that this was no ordinary mortal. He looked closely at her and saw that she was his own granddaughter. He cried, "Arise, my child. Why did you come to visit me without my knowledge? I have always warned your parents to inform me when to expect visits from you. Had I known you were coming I would have cleaned my cave."

Kaanaelike was angry and without replying she struck the side of the cave with such force that all the hangings and decorations fell from the walls.

The king cried, "What an angry granddaughter I have here. See, you have knocked from the walls the sacred bones of your ancestors."

These words drove away anger from her heart, and Kaanaelike sat on the sacred lap of her grandfather, who inquired what great object had brought her to him. She told him that she had come to gain his permission to marry the man who had come to her island from the sea.

The king was silent for a few minutes before replying, "Neither you nor your parents brought that man to your island. I sent him there. I saw him swimming in the sea. The signs of a high chief were hovering over him and I knew he would be a suitable husband for you. So I rolled Ulukaa up to him. Therefore, go back and take him as your husband. Do not make him work for you, for I shall take your life if you do."

Kaanaelike answered her grandfather thus: "All you say is good. I shall obey all your commands. But I have power as well as you. If I promise to obey you, you must likewise promise to obey me. You must not eat any more people."

"That is only fair, my granddaughter." answered the king.

At once he went to his guards and told them to release the victims from the pot, to send them home, and then to go home themselves. Then he returned to his granddaughter, who asked where the path to her island lay. The king took his tongue from the side of the cave and fastened it in his mouth. Taking her sacred pa-u with her, Kaanaelike sat on the crook of the tongue, while the giant slowly lowered her to the Rolling Island. As soon as she was safely home the tongue disappeared.

Kaanaelike hastened to her parents to tell them the outcome of her visit. She told them how her grandfather had rolled her island up to the man struggling in the sea, and had selected him as a husband for her whom they must all obey.

Her parents said, "Now great happiness dwells with us. If your grandfather had refused to allow you to marry the Man-from-the-sea, we would have given him to your younger sister."

The marriage of Kaanaelike and Kaeweaoho was celebrated by a great luau.

During the years that Kaeweaoho had ruled his people on Hawaii his fame had spread to all the islands, for he had cared tenderly for his subjects and had given them a wise and just rule.

At his disappearance his bird sisters had flown over the world hunting for him. At last, after he had been married to Kaanaelike for six months, they found him on Ulukaa. As he lay on the sand they cast him into deep sleep. A dream came to him. He heard a voice saying, "You are living in peace with your beautiful wife while your people far away are going up and down the land mourning for you. Your sacred temple has been desecrated; your bundles of tapa have been used by evil ones; your *awa* has been drunk: your sacred landing has been used; your parents mourn so that they are no longer able to eat, and sleep comes not often to them. O King, beloved by all, sleep now, but when you awake return to your land for which you had such great aloha."

When Kaeweaoho awoke he was surprised to find that he had heard this voice in a dream. Three times the same dream came to him. He became very heavy-hearted. He wanted to return to Hawaii, but he had no canoe. Hourly this dream, like an image, haunted him. As he remembered his aged, grief-stricken parents and his unhappy subjects, tears filled his eyes.

When his wife noticed his sad demeanor, she cried, "O my Man-from the-Sea, why do your tears flow? Have my parents been unkind to you?"

To these words her husband replied, "Your parents have not been unkind to me. I weep because I pine for my native land. On your island I am called the Man-from-the-Sea. In my land I am a great king. The island of Hawaii is my kingdom."

Kaanaelike went weeping to her parents and told them that her husband was the king of Hawaii, and that grief because of this treatment on their island filled her heart.

Her parents knew that the king of Hawaii was called Kaeweaoho. They told their daughter to ask her husband his name. If he replied "Kaeweaoho," she would know that he was not deceiving her.

As soon as Kaanaelike asked her husband this question he answered, "In your land I am called the Man-from-the-Sea. In my land I am called Kaeweaoho, King of Hawaii."

Then Kaanaelike's parents knew that their daughter was not deceived, for they had heard much of the wise and just rule of this king.

Kaanaelike begged her husband not to return to Hawaii. "Wait until old age dims our eyes before you leave me for your native land," she wept.

Her husband answered, "Hawaii calls me. My people need me. I shall go. If a son is born to us call him Eye-Brows-Burnt-Off, Na-kne-maka-pauikeahi. If a daughter is born to us you may name her as it pleases you. My love for you is great, but I cannot remain here. I must return to my people and my country."

By these words the unhappy Kaanaelike knew that her husband would leave her, and so she prepared to carry out his wishes. She ordered a canoe to be built for him. This canoe was to be built in one day, cut in the early morning, and ready for the sea by sunset. This canoe was to be red, with a red mast, red sails, red ropes, and the sailors were to be dressed in red tapa.

At sunset Kaeweaoho and his sailors got into the canoe. Kaanaelike warned them not to look back lest some dire calamity befall them on their journey. As the canoe glided over the sea, Kaanaelike rolled her island along close to it until she saw the waves breaking on the shores of Hawaii. Then she rolled her island back into the sea. Kaeweaoho looked back and saw only the vast water.

As Kaeweaoho approached his sacred landing he heard the crowd crying, "The *kapu* is broken. Now anyone can use the king's landing." Then he knew that his dream was true.

When the people saw Kaeweaoho they at once recognized their lost king, and with tears of joy they rushed to the sea, and, seizing the canoe, carried it into the palace yard on their shoulders, with the king and all the sailors in it. Before the palace they lowered the canoe. The king gave his great aloha to all. He entered his home, and greeted his parents and all his chiefs, whom he found living in filth and want, mourning his long absence.

Kaewenoho issued a proclamation saying that all the sacred places which had been desecrated should be returned to their *kapu* or again set apart, and that all lands set aside for the king's use should be reserved for him as before. He then sent his messengers to find and bring before him the two fishermen who had deserted him at sea.

The messengers easily found these men, for they had not heard of the king's return. When they were brought before the king they knew him to be the one they had left to die in the deep sea. Terror filled their hearts.

The king spoke to them in these words, "Why did you leave me at sea when I swam for the paddles? Were you angry with me? Had I done you any wrong?"

The terrified men answered, "Yes, you had done us a great wrong. Day after day, while we were fishing for you, no food was left at our homes by your orders."

These words greatly troubled the king. He sent for his head steward who allotted each man's food. When the steward came before the king he crawled on his hands and knees. He could not reply to the king's questions, and so he was ordered to be put to death. The king left the punishment of his fishermen to his subjects. They sentenced them to die also. So the three men were executed that day.

After Kaeweaoho had departed from Ulukaa, Kaanaelike was very troubled. She wondered what she would say to her child when it asked for its father. After her husband had been gone three years a son was born to the queen, whom she named Eye-Brows-Burnt-Off. When he was two days old he could walk, and when three days old he could talk. On the sixth day of his life he could play *ke'a-pua*[2] with the large boys. That day he said to his mother, "Where is my father?"

Kaanaelike replied, "You have no father."

---

2. This game is described in the legend of Menehune.

WILLIAM HYDE RICE

Her son replied, "Yes, I must have a father. Was I not named Eye-Brows-Burnt-Off because my father burned off his eyebrows making an *imu*?"

Then Kaanaelike knew that her secret had been made known to her son and she told him that his father was the king of Hawaii.

Eye-Brows-Burnt-Off wanted to seek his father at once. His mother told him that he could go when the canoe returned from Hawaii. Kaanaelike read the signs in the heavens and knew that her son would die if he went to Hawaii. This she told him but he only replied, "If I go to seek my father and die, it is well. If I live it is well."

So Kaanaelike prepared the canoe for her son as she had prepared it for her husband. As the boy entered it she cried to him, "Go and find your father. Give him my aloha. I fear you will never see him. You will be killed by his subjects. Do not look back. Let nothing stop you until you reach your father."

Then she followed the canoe with her rolling island until she could see the sacred landing of the king.

When the people on shore saw a red canoe nearing the beach they cried, "Kill anyone who attempts to land. No man, woman, or child shall desecrate the king's landing place."

As Eye-Brows-Burnt-Off came closer to land he said to his sailors, "Paddle no farther. I shall go ashore alone. If I am killed, return at once to Ulukaa. If I die it is well. If I reach land safely I shall build a fire. If the smoke blows towards the sea I live. If it blows towards land I die."

After he had spoken these words, the boy jumped into the sea and swam ashore. Someone tore off his clothes, but he jumped on the heads of the people standing close together in the crowd, and ran on them until he reached the gate to the palace yard. There, Eye-Brows-Burnt-Off tried to slip past the guards, who had the power of life and death over anyone entering the yard. One kindly guard wanted to let the child pass, but the other guard struck him as he ran by.

Eye-Brows-Burnt-Off breathlessly entered the rooms where his father was sleeping. Twelve kahili bearers were gently waving their kahili over the sleeping king. As the boy sprang up and sat on his father's lap the priest, who had mystic powers, recognized him as the king's son and warned the attendants to treat him well. When the king awoke he said, "Who is this on my lap?"

The boy answered, "I am Eye-Brows-Burnt-Off. You wife, Kaanaelike, sent her aloha to you. Behold, I am wounded at the hands of your people."

Kaeweaoho was very angry to think that anyone had laid hands on his son, and quickly ordered any person who had harmed him to be put to death. The unkind guard and many others were executed. At last Eye-Brows-Burnt-Off begged his father not to kill anymore.

The king then prepared a great feast for his son from Ulukaa. As they lit the *imu* the smoke rose and was swept to the sea by the breeze from the mountains. Thus the paddlers knew that their master lived.

When the feast was spread and all were seated, Eye-Brows-Burnt-Off said, "I cannot enjoy this luau. My faithful paddlers are still at sea. I had forgotten them."

The king sent at once for these men, who were given places at the feast, where they were treated as honored guests by all the chiefs of Hawaii. After the meal, they were sent to the houses they had occupied on their former visit to Hawaii, when they had brought the king home.

When evening came, Eye-Brows-Burnt-Off told his father that at sun rise on the following day he would return to Ulukaa. The king urged him to stay with him but the boy answered, "If I remain you will die. My mother has gathered all her sisters together to try you. After I am gone you must build eleven houses for them. They will come here and each one will pretend that she is your wife. You must send each one to the house you have prepared for her. When the youngest sister, Keahiwela, who is the most beautiful, comes, you will think that she is your wife. You must tell her that even her whole body is not as beautiful as your wife's eyes. Kaanaelike will be the last to come ashore. If she sits on your lap and kisses you, you will know that she is your wife, and your life will be spared. If you do not do as I say, death will be your fate."

Early the next morning Eye-Brows-Burnt-Off got into his canoe and started for Ulukaa. As they neared the Rolling Island the boy saw the eleven beautiful women. His mother was looking at them from the top of her house. She was preparing to go to Hawaii to avenge the injuries done her son by her husband's subjects.

As soon as the boy stepped ashore, the beautiful women got into the canoe. Kaanaelike was the last to enter. She moved the Rolling Island close to Hawaii. Just at daybreak her island disappeared, and with her sisters concealed in the canoe, the angry queen paddled toward the shore. When the natives saw the canoe coming to the king's sacred landing they cried, "The canoe comes which took the prince away. A woman is paddling it."

After the canoe had reached the shore one of the beautiful sisters stepped on land. The people cried, "What a beautiful woman. She must be the king's wife. Take her to the palace."

But the king remembering his son's words, said, "She is not my wife. Lead her to her house."

When the sixth sister stepped ashore the people cried, "This is your wife. Admit her to the palace. There are no more beautiful women in the canoe."

She looked so much like Kaanaelike that even the king thought she was his wife, but his *kahuna* warned him, "Take her not. She is not your wife. If you admit her you will die. The sea will cover your land."

She was sent to her house.

When the youngest sister came, the king was certain she was his wife. But as before his *kahuna* warned him to remember his son's words. So she was sent to her house, having first been told that her beauty could not compare with that of Kaanaelike.

At last Kaanaelike came to the palace of her king. Her beauty was as blinding as the sun. The people were unable to look upon her. Then Kaeweaoho knew that she was his wife. His son had spoken truthfully, and a great aloha for the boy filled the father's heart. Kaanaelike sat on her husband's lap and kissed him, and he knew that he would live.

Kaanaelike made known her plans. She said that when the sun rose on the following day, the king should return with her to Ulukaa. The king agreed to this. At sunrise the king and queen paddled away from Hawaii, which was left in the hands of Kaeweaoho's father. The father ruled until all the chiefs of Hawaii had died. At his own death, the kingdom passed into the hands of twins from Kauai.

After Kannaelike and her husband had reached Ulukaa, the queen sent all her sisters home to their own islands except the youngest sister, Keahiwela, Hot-Fire, who lived with her by the sea.

In a short time Kaanaelike saw that her husband was paying too much attention to her beautiful sister, so she took him to live under the watchful eye of her parents.

One day the king asked permission to go fishing. His wife prepared his bait and fishing lines. He went to the sea and caught twelve fish. Before going home he went to the home of his wife's sister. He wakened her, but she warned him to go away, or his wife with her supernatural powers would see him. The king listened to her and departed, leaving her seven of the fish.

Towards evening the king returned home with the other five fish. Kaanaelike felt the fish and seeing that they were dry, asked her husband where he had been. He replied that the sun had been very hot, and he had walked slowly. Then his wife looked at his fishing lines and saw that twelve fish had been caught. When Kaanaelike asked where the other fish were Kaeweaoho answered that his canoe had capsized and he had lost all but the five which she had.

A few days later the king asked to go to catch birds. His wife prepared the gum for him, and he went through the forest putting gum on the flowers. Instead of waiting for the birds to come he hurried to the younger sister's house and stayed all day with her. At sunset he went home and when his wife asked for the birds he told her that he had had an unlucky day. She looked at the gum and said, "Plenty of birds have been caught but no one was there to collect them."

The next day Kaeweaoho went again to the house of the beautiful sister. This time his wife followed him. When she saw her husband and sister together, she spat between them, and fire broke out which destroyed the king and spread rapidly over the island, wiping out everything and everybody. Keahiwela turned herself into a pile of stones, so that the fire could not destroy her. Kaanaelike put out the fire to save the life of her son, Eye-Brows-Burnt-Off. When the fire was out, she saw the pile of stones and knew that her sister still lived in it.

Just at this moment the foster parents of Keahiwela, who had become greatly alarmed over her long absence, sent their dog to find her. He was named Kuilio-loa, My-Long-Dog. Everywhere this dog went, the country was polluted. With one bound he landed on Ulukaa and saw that all the people on the island had been destroyed. He returned to his master, telling him that Keahiwela was dead. The master sent him back to Ulukaa with power to kill Kaanaelike. He jumped back to the island with his mouth wide open to bite Kaanaelike. Keahiwela saw him and, shaking off the rocks that covered her, jumped into the dog's mouth.

When Kaanaelike saw the dog with bloody teeth she took her sacred pa-u and struck him, cutting off his tail and ears. From that day to this bob-tailed dogs have lived on the islands. This dog took Keahiwela home to her parents, and then he jumped across to Kauai where he lived until his death. When Eye-Brows-Burnt-Off saw all that had happened on Ulukaa, he said to his mother, "You have brought all this trouble to the land. There are no people left for me to rule over. I shall go to someother land where there are people. You must live here alone to the end of your life."

The old Hawaiians believe that Kaanaelike still lives on the Rolling Island, Ulukaa, which can be seen, a cloud-like vision, with the other eleven islands, on the horizon at sunrise or at sunset. At sunrise the island of Ulukaa has a reddish tinge, which shows that it is still burning. Because they are sacred islands, it is bad luck to point at them.

The Stones of Kane

A Legend of Kauai

In the beginning, a woman and her two brothers, Pohakuloa and Pohaku, in the form of stones, came through the water from distant lands. When they reached the reef off Haena the sister wanted to stay there, but one of the brothers urged her to go on, saying, "If you stay here the *limu* will cover you, the *opihi* will cling to you, and the people coming to fish will climb over you."

To this the sister replied, "If you go into the mountains the birds will light on you and the lizards will crawl over you."

So the sister stayed in the sea where at low tide she is still to be seen. The Hawaiians call the rock O-o-aa, the Fast-Rooted. The brothers swam towards land. When about two hundred yards inland from the shore one became tired and lay down to rest, and there he can be seen to this day lying, covered with moss, among the *puhala* trees. He is called Pohakuloa, Long-Stone. The sand beneath Pohakuloa was used as a burial place for common people. The other brother went on and began to climb up the steep mountain side. The great god, Kane, saw him and, taking pity on him, threw him up on the top of the ridge where he is today known as the Stone of Kane, Pohaku-o-Kane.

The Menehune

A Legend of Kauai

THE BELIEF OF THE HAWAIIANS of ancient times was that there was one great continent, stretching from Hawaii, including Samoa, Lalakoa, and reaching as far as New Zealand, also taking in Fiji. And there were some lowlands in between these higher lands. All this was called by one name, that is Ka-houpo-o-Kane, the Solar-Plexus-of-Kane (the great god), and was also called Moana-mui-kai-oo, the Great-Engulfing-Ocean. This is the same that is mentioned in the prayer used by the kahuna ana-ana, who can pray to death, and who can also defend from death, when they pray in these words to ward off the evil that is keeping the sick one down:

To You, Who are the Breath of the Eighth Night:
To You, Kane, the Yellow Edge of Night:
To You Kane, the Thunder that Rumbles at Night:
To You, Kane, Kamoloalii, Brother of Pele, Sea of Forgiveness:
To You, Ku, Kane, and all the other Gods that hold up the Heavens:
And likewise the Ku, the Goddess women that hold up the Night:
To You, Kane, Who is bristling, to Ku, and to Lono:
To You, Lono, Who is awakening as the sun rises:
To All of You in the Night: Stand up!
Let the Night pass, and Daylight come to me, the **Kahuna**
Look at our sick one: If he be dying from food eaten in the day,
Or from tapa, or from what he has said,
Or from pleasures he has had a part in,
Or from walking on the highway.
From walking, or from sitting down,
Or from the bait that has been taken,
Or from parts of food that he has left,
Or from his evil thoughts of others,
Or from finding fault, or from evils within,
From all deaths: Deliver and forgive!
Take away all great faults, and all small faults,
Throw them all into Moana-nui-kai-oo, the great ocean!
If Ku is there, or Hina: Hold back death!

> *Let out the big life, the small life,*
> *Let out the long life, for all time:*
> *That is the life from the Gods.*
> *This is the ending of my prayer*
> *It is finished; **Amama ua noo**.*

This is what they thought in regard to the land of Ka-houpo-o-Kane, which is related in the most ancient tradition, that has been handed down for countless generations, the tradition known as "Ke Kumulipo," "the tradition that comes from the Dark Ages."

The great flood came, Kai-a-ka-hina-alii, the Sea-that-Made-the-Chiefs Fall-Down (that destroyed the chiefs), submerging all the lower lands, leaving only specks of higher land, now known as islands, above the waters. The lower lands were covered by Moana-nui-kai-oo. Nim, a powerful *kahuna*, saved a great many people.

After the deluge there were three peoples: the Menehune, who were dwarfs or pygmies; the Ke-na-mu and the Ke-na-wa. A great part of these other peoples were destroyed by the Menehune. One of the chiefs of the Ke-na-mu had come to Hawaii from Kahiki. The name of this chief was Kuala-nui-kini-akua, Big-Kualu-of-the-Four-Thousand-Gods. He had a son Kualu-mui-pauku-moku-moku, Big-Kuala-of-the-Broken Rope, the father of Ola, Life. They came from Kapaia-haa, otherwise called Kahiki-moe, the land that is now called New Zealand. They came to the land of Ka-ma-wae-lua-lani-nei, that is now called Kauai-a-mano-ka-lani-po. That was the land where the three peoples had their home, the Ke-na-mu, the Ke-na-wa, and the Menehune. They lived there and emigrated thence as the people of more recent times have lived and travelled. At one time the Menehune journeyed until they reached the land of Kahiki-ka-paia-haa (New Zealand). That is why some people believe that they came originally from New Zealand, but that is not so. They were natives of Hawaii.

In the ancient tradition of "Kumulipo" it is told that there were a great many men and women from Ka-houpo-o-kane who went to Kahiki-ka-paia-haa, and in those emigrations, there was one called He-ma, the progenitor of the Maori race. When He-ma went, at about that time, the Menehune people went, too, from Kauai-a-mano-ka-lani-po.

At that time Ma-oli-ku-laiakea or Maori-tu-raiatea, in the New Zealand language, was the king of the Menehune. He went with his people, accompanied by their chief, Aliikilola, and his wife, Lepoa.

This was in the time of He-ma. And from the first part of the name of the king of the Menehune, the New Zealanders called themselves Maori. From the last part of the same name a place in New Zealand is called Raiatea. That is what is told in the most ancient of all traditions, called "Ke Kumulipo."

When the Menehune returned to Kauai, they began to increase. The tribe grew until there were enough grown men to form two rows, reaching all the way from Makaweli to Wailua. They were so many, counting the women and children, that the only fish of which each could have one to himself, was the shrimp.

The Menehune were a small people, but they were broad and muscular and possessed of great strength. Contrary to common belief they were not possessed of any supernatural powers, but it was solely on account of their tremendous strength and energy and their great numbers that they were able to accomplish the wonderful things they did. These pygmy people were both obedient and industrious, always obeying their leaders. Their average height was only from two feet, six inches, to three feet, but they were intelligent and well organized. They took no food from other lands, but cultivated enough for themselves. As they were hard workers, they always had plenty of food. Their favorite foods were *haupia*, a pudding made of arrowroot, sweetened with coconut milk; *pala-ai*, the squash, and *ko-ele-pa-lau*, or sweet potato pudding. They were also very fond of luau, the cooked young leaves of the taro, fern-fronds, and other greens. They had elaborately made and carved wooden dishes and utensils for their food.

One curious thing about the Menehune was that they never worked in daylight, as they never wanted to be seen. It was their rule that any enterprise they undertook had to be finished in a single night. If this could not be done they never returned to that piece of work. Being such a strong people, they almost always finished the task in one night. It is not known where their houses were, but it is said that they lived in eaves and hollow logs, and as soon as it began to be daylight, they all disappeared. One great thing that they did was to cultivate the wild taro, either on the *pali* or in the swamps, for they planted anywhere they could find room for a single plant.

On the cliffs of Kauai are still seen many paths and roads which were built by them, and which are still called Ke-ala-pii-a-ka-Menehune, the Trails-of-the-Menehune. These trails are still to be seen above Hanapepe, Makaweli, Mana, Napali, Milolii, Nualolo and Hanapu. In the little hollows on the cliffs, they planted wild taro, yams, ferns, and bananas. No cliff was too steep for them to climb.

They also built many heiaus, including those of Elekuna, Polihale, and Kapa-ula, near Mana, Malae at Wailua, on the Lihue side of the river, just above the road, and Poli-ahu on the high land, between the branching of the Wailua river and the Opai-kaa stream. All the stones for these heiaus were brought from Makaweli. The Menehune formed two lines, and passed the stones from man to man. They also built the heiau at Kiha-wahine on Niihau. It is built of coral rock and is oblong in shape, with two corners fenced in as *kapu* places; one for the sacrificial altar, and the other for *kahuna*, or high priest.

The Menehune hewed out two stone canoes, which were called by the Hawaiians, Waa-o-kau-meli-eli. These canoes, covered with earth, are still to be found at the Mana side of the Waimea Hotel.

At one time the Menehune hollowed out a huge stone, and carried it to Waimea, where the head Menehune fisherman used it as a house. It was called Papa-ena-ena, from his name. He sat in this house, and watched his men fish.

It was their custom to place in the streams big stones on which to pound their food. One of these big stones is to be seen far up the Hanalei River. Another was carried from Mahaulepu across Kipukai to Holes. Still another was placed near the mountain of Maunahina in a little brok above Wainiha, where to this day, natives leave offerings of lehua branches to the *kupua*, or demi-god, of the locality. On this stone, Lahi and his son lived, after Lahi had been defeated in Waimea. His story is told in the legend of "The Bird Man." From his life came the saying. "Tear the bird, the water is rippling." The explanation of this proverb is that if anyone stepped into the brook, the ripples could be seen along its whole course. Therefore, when the water rippled, the boy knew that someone was wading through the stream, and said, "Tear the bird," meaning, "Eat at once," so that they would be prepared, in case it were the enemy approaching.

At one time the Menehune built two canoes of koa in the mountains near Pun-la-Pele. As they were dragging them down to the lowlands, they were caught by a heavy rain-storm, and were forced to leave the canoes across the little valley. The storm covered the canoes with debris, and later, a road was built across them, over which all the materials to build the village of Waimea were hauled.

While these canoes were being placed in this valley one of the Menehune broke a law, and was condemned to die. He was turned into a stone which is still called Poha'-kina-pua'a, and can be seen on the Waimea Canyon road, not far below Pun-la-Pele. As the stone was being placed, such a shout was raised that it frightened the ducks on the Kawainui pond near Kailua, on Oahu. At Mahaulepu, on Kanai, another Menehune was turned to stone for stealing watermelons. The Menehune regarded a thief with great contempt, and the penalty for such a crime was death by being turned into stone.

It is believed that this happened before the Menehune left Kauai and journeyed to New Zealand. When a son, Ola, was born to the king of Waimea, the headman, Kisals-nui-pauku-moku-moku, hastened to the far-lying islands of New Zealand, and brought the Menehune back to Kauai.

After their return the Menehune built the wall of the Alakoko fishpond at Niumala. Standing in two rows they passed the stones from hand to land all the way from Makaweli to Niumalu. Daylight came before they had finished the work, and two gaps were left in the wall. These were filled in by Chinamen in late years, and the pond is still in use.

Ola, the king, obtained the promise of the Menehune that they would build a water-lead at Waimea, if all the people stayed in their houses, the dogs muzzled, and the chickens shut in calabashes, so that there would be no sound on the appointed night. This was done, and the Menehune completed the watercourse before daybreak. It has stood the storms of many years, and is still called Kiki-a-Ola, Ola's-Water-Lead.

The Menehune also carried large flat stones from Koloa to Kalalau, where they built a big heiau, which stands to this day.

The favorite sport of these small men was to jump off cliffs into the sea. They carried stones from the mountains to their bathing places, where they placed them in piles. Then, throwing a stone into the sea, the skillful swimmer would dive after it. This was repeated until all the stones had disappeared.

One of their bathing places was at Ninini, a little beach, surrounded by cliffs, just inside the point where the larger Nawiliwili lighthouse now stands. While the Menehune were carrying a large rock from Kipukai to Ninini, half of it broke off, and fell into the Huleia River, where it is still used as a bridge called Kipapa-o-ka-Menehune, the Causeway-of-the-Menehune. The other half of the rock is still at Ninini.

From Ninini the swimmers went to Homai-ka-waa, Bring-the-Canoe, the next valley beyond Kealia. While they were bathing there a very large shark almost caught A-a-ka, one of the Menehune. They all swam ashore to a plain still known as A-a-ka, where they discussed plans to get revenge. Soon all the Menehune were ordered to gather morning-glory vine, of which a large basket was made. This, filled with bait, was lowered into the sea, and the shark was caught. Then he was towed around to a reef beyond Anahola. The odor of the shark soon brought so many land and sea birds to feast upon the flesh that the reef was called A-li-o-ma-nu, Where-the-Water-is-made-still-by-the-Oil-from-the-Shark, and is still known by this name.

The Menehune never again bathed at Ho-mai-ka-waa, but they built there the big heiau where Kawelo worshipped his shark god. The story of Kawelo is told in the legend of that name. They also erected a pile of stones at A-li-o-ma-nu in memory of their delivery from the shark. This pile of stones is called Ka-hua-a-li-ko.

At Molowaa, the Dry-Canoe, stones were piled up, and a bathing place called Uluoma was made. While the men were bathing there, the *luna*, or head man, saw that one Menehune, named Maliu, was missing. He quickly sent out a searching party. In the meantime the missing one, who had been visiting at some Hawaiian home, saw the searchers, and began digging at the spot where a spring came out from a coral rock. There he was found, and he explained that he had discovered this spring, where they could all drink good water. So his life was spared. The spring was called Ka-wai-a-Maliu, the Water-of-Maliu, and is still to be seen.

Traveling on, the Menehune moved a big stone to Kahili, below Kilauea, which they used to dive from. At Mokuaeae, the island off the present Kilauea lighthouse, they began to fill in the channel between the island and the mainland. They were just able to touch the bottom with a paddle when morning dawned, and their task was left unfinished.

Near Kalihiwai a cave was dug, called Wa-ka-ulua. This became a well-known spot for catching ulua. At Hanalei, a large narrow stone, called Lani-ho-eho, Brushed-off-the-Heavens, was placed near the point of Pooku by one of the little men, none of his companions being willing to help him. At the point of Kealahula, at Lumahai, these wonderful men made a small hill on the seashore, by cutting off part of the point. You can still see the bare place on the ridge, where the earth was sliced off. At the base of this small hill, the Menehune placed a large stone, which they used as a jumping-off place. The hill is called Ma-ka-ihu-waa, the Landing Place-of-the-Canoes.

On the plain above the Lumalai River the Menehune made their homes for a time. There one of the small men began to build a heiau which he called Ka-i-li-o-o-pa-ia. As he was working, the big owl of Kane came and sat on the stones. This bird was large enough to carry off a man, and naturally, it frightened away the little workman. He returned next day, only to see the huge bird flying over the spot, croaking. He also saw the great monster dog. Kuilio-loa, My-Long-Dog, running about the heiau. These evil omens caused the Menehune to believe that the heiau was polluted, so he gave up his work.

One day, as the Menehane were bathing at Lumahai, one of them caught a large ulua. The fish tried to escape, but the little man struggled bravely, and finally killed it. The man was so badly wounded, however, that his blood flowed over the spot, and turned the earth and stones red. This place is still called Ka-a-le-le, from the name of the wounded man.

Weli, a bow-legged, deep-voiced Menehune *konohiki*, king's sheriff or executor, is remembered as an agriculturist. On the plain of Lumahai he planted breadfruit trees, which are there to this day. They were called Na-ulu-a-Weli, after the Menehune.

The small explorers soon found their way to the head of the Lunahai Valley, whence they crossed over to Wainiha. There they found an immense rock, one side of which was gray, and the other black. This they hewed out into the shape of a poi board, and placed it near the falls of the Lumahai River. To this day, the *wi*, or freshwater shellfish, come out on the gray side in the day-time, and on the black side at night. Even now no woman can successfully fish there unless she wears a certain lei of shredded ti leaves or breaks off two lehua branches, crying to the *kapua*, as she throws one to the *mauki* side, or toward the mountains, and one to the makai side, or toward the sea, "Pa-na-a-na-a, give us luck!" If a man fishes there, he first throws two small stones into the water, asking for success.

The next nocturnal enterprise of these little men was to span the river with a bridge of flat stones, but freshets have since removed all traces of this work.

During their stay at Lumalai one of the Menehune who was skilled in stone carving, tried to escape by climbing up the cliffs towards Waialeale. The *kononiki* sent his men to capture him. They overtook him at about the middle of the cliff, and the usual punishment was meted out to him his body was turned into stone and placed on the spot where he was captured. It is there today, a huge stone in the form of a man with a gray body and a white head. The path the pursuers followed zigzags up the steep *pali* to the stone, which is called Ma-i-na-ke-ha-u, the Man-Out of-Breath.

The Menehune then went on to Wainihi, where they placed a stone in the middle of the ridge, leaving such a narrow space to pass that in after years the Hawaiians had to hold on to the stone, and make themselves as small as possible in order to edge around it. So the stone be came known as the "Hungry Stone." In the Wainiha River a flat stone was placed which reaches from bank to bank, and part of which is always above water.

Hurrying on to the top of Kilohana, the Menehune built on the plain there a little hill about ten feet high called Po-po-pii. There they amused themselves by rolling down its slopes. They made so much noise at this sport that the birds at Kahuku, on Oahu, were frightened.

Ka-u-ki-u-ki, the Angry-one, a Menehune, declared that he could go to the top of this hill and catch the legs of the moon. This boast was ridiculed, and when he was unable to carry it out, he was turned into stone. This stone was often covered with maile and lehua branches by the natives, so that the rain and fog would not prevent their carrying out their plans.

In the valley of Lanihuli the Menehune lived for sometime, planting it with different varieties of plants which are still there. Several times Hawaiians tried to steal their food, and were always turned into stone on the spot where they were overtaken.

After they had been living in this valley for sometime the king found that many of his men were marrying Hawaiian women. This worried him greatly as he was anxious to keep his race pure. At last he decided to leave the islands. Summoning his counselors, his astrologers, and his leading men, he told them his plans. They agreed with their king, and a proclamation was issued calling all the Menehune together on the night of the full moon.

On the appointed night such a crowd gathered on the plain of Ma-hi-e that the vegetation there was trampled down, and the place, to this day, is barren.

There, in the moonlight, the king saw all the Menehune and their firstborn sons, and he addressed them with these words, "My people, you whom I love, I have called you together to explain my plans for leaving this island. I desire that we keep our race distinct from others, and in order to do this we must go to other lands. You must leave behind you, your wives chosen from the Hawaiian race. You may take with you only your older sons. The food we have planted in this valley is ripe. It shall be left for your wives."

As soon as the king had finished speaking, a man called Mo-hi-ki-a said, "We have heard your words, O King. I have married a Hawaiian woman and we have a son grown to manhood. I have taught him all the skill I possess in making stone and koa canoes. He can polish them as well as hew them out. I beg you to take him in my place. He holds in his right hand the stone adz for making stone canoes, and in his left hand the adz for koa canoes. I have had mighty strength. No stone was too large for me to move. No tree was too tall for me to cut down and make into a canoe. My son has strength, as I have had. Take him in my place. If at anytime you need me, send a messenger for me. My son can be that messenger. He has been taught to run."

Having heard this request, Kii-la-mi-ki, the speaker of the Menehune, rose and answered in this manner: "You who beg to be left behind to live with your Hawaiian wife, listen! That woman has only lately come into your life. The king has always been in your life. We see your firstborn there, but none of us have seen him work, and we do not know what he can do. You say that you have taught him all you know in canoe building, but we have never seen him work. We do not know that he can take your place. We all feel that you must go with us."

These words were echoed by a great chorus from the crowd: "He shall not stay! He shall go!"

When at last the Menehune were quieted, they heard the voice of the high sheriff saying, "One word from the king, and we shall obey in everything. It is only by listening to his words, and by obeying him that our race shall be kept together. Otherwise rebellion will come. All must be done as he says."

Then a great stillness fell upon the assembled people. The herald of the king rose, and cried out, "Let no word be spoken! Words are *kapu*. *Meha meha*, be absolutely still! The heavens speak through the voice of your king. Lie down on your faces before him!"

After seeing these signs of his people's obedience the king rose and said, "Listen, my people, to these words which shall come from my mouth. I deny the request of Mo-hi-ki-a. I ask you not to leave him behind. We shall start on our way tomorrow night. Take only what food you need for a few days. Leave all the growing crops for the Hawaiian women you have taken as wives, lest criticism fall upon us. Before we depart I wish a monument to be erected to show that we have lived here."

As soon as the people had heard these words they began to build a pile of stones on the top of the mountain. When they had finished their work they placed a grooved stone on top, as a monument to the Menehune king and his leaders. Not far from it was dug a square hole, with caves in its sides. This was the monument to the Menehune of common birth.

When these last works of their hands were completed, the little men raised such a great shout that the fish in the pond of Nomilu, across the island, jumped in fright, and the moi, the wary fish, left the beaches.

The rest of the night was used by the *konohiki*, who separated the men into twenty divisions of sixteen thousand each. The women were divided into eight divisions of twenty thousand each. Besides these, there were ten thousand half-grown boys, and of girls up to the age of seventeen there were ten thousand six hundred. Each division was placed under a leader. The work of the first division was to clear the road of logs, and similar obstructions. That of the second was to lower the hills. The third was to sweep the path. Another division had to carry the sleds and sleeping mats, for the king. One division had charge of the food and another of the planting. One division was composed of *kahuna*, soothsayers, and astrologers. Still another was made up of storytellers, fun-makers, minstrels, and musicians, who furnished amusement for the king. Some of the musicians played the nose-flute, which was one and a half spans long, and half an inch in diameter, and made of bamboo. One end was closed, and about two inches below, was the hole into which they breathed, and blew out the music. About the middle of the flute was another hole which they fingered, to make the different notes. Others blew the ti-leaf trumpets, which were made by ripping a ti leaf part away along the middle ridge, and rolling over the torn piece. Through this they blew, varying the sound by fingering. Others played crude stringed instruments of pliable black hau wood with strings of tough olo-na fiber. These, called *ukeke*, they held in their mouths, and twanged the strings, with their fingers. Still others beat drums of shark skin, stretched taut over the ends of hollow tree trunks.

When all was arranged, orders were given for starting the following night.

At the appointed time the Menehune set forth. Many obstructions were found but each division did its work of cutting, clearing, and sweeping the path. They also planted wild taro, yams, and other food-producing plants all along the way. After they had climbed to the top of the mountain, they encamped at a placed called Kanaloa-huluhulu, the Hairy Devil, and sent men back to fish.

It happened that while they were resting there one of the chiefesses, Hanakapiai, gave birth to a child. When the child was a week old the mother died. Her body was turned into stone, and a valley was named after her. A few days later another chiefess, Hanakeao, stepped on a stone, which rolled down into the next valley, hurling her to death. That valley bears the name of the unfortunate one. As these women had been dearly loved, the king ordered a period of mourning which was to last sixty days. During that time no sports were to be indulged in.

All the fishermen were sent back to Haena to fish. There they found a great many small fish, so many in fact, that they could not carry all. So they took part of the catch, and left them on the plain, near the *pali*. When they returned with the remainder of the fish, they saw that the *akua* had stolen all the first half, and had disappeared through a hole in the mountain. The fishermen divided into two groups, one following the thieves into the hole, and the other beginning to dig a cave near the supposed outlet of the hole. In a short time a huge cave was dug, and then they came upon the offending *akua* who were promptly put to death. This dry cave is still to be seen at Haena, and the natives call it Maniniholo, after the head fisherman of the Menehune, or Kahauna, from the smell of the dead bodies of the akua.

When at last the sixty days of mourning were ended, the king ordered the *ilamoku*, the marshal, to proclaim a big feast to be followed by sports of many kinds.

Some of these were: spinning tops, or *olo-hu*, made of small gourds or kukui nuts, or sometimes carved of wiliwili wood, boxing, wrestling, and similar games such as *uma*, or *kulakulai*. This was played by the two opponents stretching at full length, face down, on the ground, with their heads together, and their bodies in opposite directions. Each leaned on his right elbow, and grasped the other's right hand, firmly. Then each tried to twist the other's arm back, until the back of his opponent's hand touched the ground, meantime keeping his own body flat on the ground. This game could be played with the left hand, as well as with the right.

They also played *maika*, a game resembling discus throwing, played with evenly-rounded, perfectly balanced stones, from two to eight inches across, and thicker in the middle than on the edge. On Kauai the *maika* were made of black stone, but on the other islands they were generally of sandstone. They were always highly polished. The *maika* were thrown to see how far they would go, but sometimes the men would race with the *maika*.

Another game they played was *ke'a-pua*, in which they took the straight shafts of the sugar cane tassels, and shot them like arrows from a whip like contrivance. This was made of a stick about three feet long, with a string five or six feet long, attached. The end of this string, doubled over, was folded around the shaft, and the remainder wound around smoothly and evenly, so as not to catch. The shaft was laid on the ground, with the point a little raised, and then whipped off. If it was well-balanced, it flew several hundred feet. The person whose *ke'a-pua* shot furthest, won, and he kept his arrow, which was called Hia-pai-ole, the Arrow-which-could-not-be-Beaten.

The queen's favorite game was *puhenchene*. This was played by placing five piles of tapa on the ground. A little flat stone, called the *noa*, was hidden in one of the piles, while the opponent watched the nimble fingers and movements of the arm muscles of his rival. Then he had to guess under which pile it was hidden, and point his stick at it. The queen usually won from the king, laughing at him, thus giving the game its name, which means "jeering."

Another sport was the tug-of-war. When one side was about to be beaten, others jumped in, and helped them. On the ninth and tenth nights of their celebration the Menehune had footraces. In these, two Menehune raced at a time. The two last to race were Pakia and Luhau. These were known to be so swift that they could run around Kauai six times in one day. Pakia won the race, beating Luhau by three fathoms. The people stood up and cheered when the decision was given, and picked up the champion, and carried him on their shoulders.

The next night they were to have sled races. They were to race down the steep hillside of a little valley that leads into Hanakapiai. If the course for the races was not slippery enough, they covered it with very fine rushes to make the sleds slide easily and swiftly. The first to race were Pahukon and Pohaha. The sled of Pabuku tipped, and he was thrown off, so Pohaha reached the goal first, and won the race. The next race was between two women, who were noted for their skill, Kapa'i, and Mukea. Kapa'i won this race, and Mukea joined in cheering her opponent. Next came a race between Mohihi, the queen, and Manu, a chief. Mohihi

WILLIAM HYDE RICE

won, by only half a length, and Manu joined in the applause. The king and all the chiefs were very much pleased that the queen had won the race. It was a great thing for her to beat Manu, for he was supposed to be the champion of all the Menehune people. That was the last of the races.

Then the father of Manu came to the king, and suggested that they make a big pile of stones at this spot, as a monument. Then all the Menehunes clapped their hands, and agreed to do so. There was great rejoicing among them, and so they built up a huge pile of stones, which they finished just as daybreak. Then the Menehune left that place, and traveled on their way.

The Story of Ola

AS WE HAVE ALREADY BEEN told, the king of the Ke-na-mu on Kauai-a-mano-ka-lani-po, was Kualu-mui-pauku-moku-moku, Big-Kualu-of-the Broken-Rope. While he was living in Waimea, he met and fell in love with a beautiful princess, Kuhapuola, who had come from Peapea, above Hana pepe, on the Waimea side. At length, after having spent many happy days with her, the king decided to return to his kingly duties at Kekaha. He called the lovely girl to his side, and gave her his *malo* and *lei palaoa*, a necklace of many braided strands of human hair, fastened by a hooked ivory ornament. This could be worn only by high chiefs, and was one of the signs of royalty. He told her that if a boy were born to her, she should name him after the king's family, but if a girl were born, she might select the name herself.

After a time the princess gave birth to a boy, whom she called Kualu-nui, as she had been told. As the child grew older he became very mischievous and headstrong. He refused to regard the *kapu* of the *kahuna* and was always in trouble.

At one time the people had gathered to make a *kahe* or fish-trap in the Makaweli River to catch the fish which the freshet would carry down.

An order was issued that no one was to touch the *kahe* until the *kahuna* had removed the *kapu*. But the boy disregarded this order and ate of the fish that had been caught. In great anger the kahuna caught him, and took him to *kahuna*, where he was tried the following day before the king.

Hearing that her son was in trouble, the princess hurried to her kahuna, asking what she should do to save her boy. The *kahuna* answered,

"Take the *malo* and the *lei palaoa* of the king and six kukui nuts. You must walk to Kekaha, and as you go you must be ever tossing the six nuts into the air and catching them. If you drop one, your child will die. If you catch all, his life will be spared." The princess at once set out for Kekaha. Her journey was successful, for not once did she let fall a nut.

When she came into the presence of the king, who was sitting in the heiau of Hauola, she saw her son bound, ready to be offered as a sacrifice, for his crime of breaking the sacred *kapu*. Going before the king, she showed him his *malo* and *lei palaoa*. He at once recognized the princess and spared the life of his son whom he called Ola, or Life, and named him as his successor.

Upon the death of the king, Ola succeeded to the kingdom. His first thought was for his people whose troubles he well know. They had had a great deal of difficulty in bringing the water from the Waimea River down to their taro patches in the Waimea flats, as none of their flumes had lasted.

Wishing to remove this trouble Ola consulted his *kahuna*, Pi, who gave him this advice: "Establish a *kapu* so that no one can go out of his house at night. Then I shall summon the Menehune to build a stone water-lead around the point of the Waimea River so that your people will always have an abundant water supply."

Ola established the *kapu*. No man, woman, or child was to go out of his house at night. Then Pi summoned the Menehune to come from foreign lands and make the water-lead in one night.

Beforehand Pi had arranged the stones in a cliff, every one of the same size and shape. From this cliff each Menehune took one stone which he called Haawe-a-Pi, the Pack-of-Pi, and placed it in the lead. This water course is still called Kiki-a-Ola, and it has stood the floods of many years.

When this task was finished a great feast was given at the heiau of Hauola. The Menehune made such a great noise that the ducks in the pond of Kawainui, at Kailua, Oahu, were frightened.

Ola next ordered the Menehune to build a large canoe house in the mountains. When it was finished they hewed out canoes, which they took to the king as he asked for them. One night as two canoes were being dragged from the mountains, they broke into two pieces and filled up the mouth of the valley of Kawaa-haki. Debris collected around the broken canoes until a road was made.

Later, Ola sent the Menehune to build a heiau at the mouth of the

Wailua River, which was to be called Hauola, after the famous city of refuge of his father at Kekaha.

The Menehune encamped above Haena on the flats which they called Kanaloa-hulu-hulu. At Ola's request they planted taro on the cliffs of Kalalau, where it is still growing. Between Kalalau and Waimea they built a big *imu*, called Kapuahi-a-Ola, and the Fire-Sacred-to-Ola.

Ola was ever thinking of improvements for his people, and his faithful laborers, the Menehune, carried them out. Many roads were built by them. One was a road of short sticks through the swamps of Alakai from Waimea to the heights above Wainiha. This road is still the only path across the otherwise impassable swamp.

The Bird Man

A Legend of Kauai

LAHI, OR LAUHAKA, AS HE is sometimes called, lived in Wainiha valley. From childhood he had refused to eat any food but the meat of birds. As he grew older the meat of small birds would not satisfy him, and so his uncle, Kanealohi, the Slow-Man, took him to the top of Kilohana, where the *uwa'u* nested. These *uwa'u* were about the size of chickens. They were gray-feathered, with white breasts, with beaks like those of seagulls. Daylight blinded them, and though they were great fishers, they always returned to their nests in the mountains before dawn. Their name comes from the sound of their call or croak, "Uwa'u." While they were in the mountains, the uncle and boy made birds' nests, so that the *uwa'u* would be well cared for.

While they were living there, a giant came who tore the nests and tried to kill the men. The boy planned to get rid of their tormentor, and explained his plan to his uncle in these words, "I shall dig a long hole in the mountain. You crawl into it, dragging with you, by its tail, a bird. When the giant reaches for the bird, you draw it a little further in. When the giant is thus caught in the hole I shall kill him." The plan was carried out, and the giant was put to death.

But, in the meantime, the king had heard that the boy and his uncle were destroying the nests of the *uwa'u*. So there was more trouble in store for them, for he had gathered together four hundred soldiers to do battle with the two bird-catchers on Kilohana.

Now Lahi and his uncle had moved to the head of a very narrow valley through which flowed a small stream. If anyone stepped into this stream at any place in its course, the water at the source would ripple. In this way a warning of the coming of friend or foe was always given, and if they were eating birds, the boy would call, "Tear the bird, Kanealohi, the water is rippling."

One day, as they were roasting birds, the boy saw the water rippling, and called out his warning. The uncle at first replied that no one was coming, but looking again, he saw the dark shadows in the water. Then, in a few minutes, they saw the king and his four hundred men advancing. In despair, Kanealohi cast himself over the cliff, but, as he was falling, the boy caught him and put him behind him out of sight.

WILLIAM HYDE RICE

The pass was so narrow that only one man could ascend at a time. And so the boy killed the soldiers, one by one, as they attempted to come up, until the four hundred were thrown over the cliff. The last one to come up was the king. He recognized the boy as his own son and begged, "Give me life in the name of your mother!"

Lahi therefore spared his life. The king thanked him with these words, "I will return to Waimea and there build a house for you. When it is finished, I shall send for you to come to me."

Returning to Waimea, the king ordered his men to dig a very deep hole. Over it, he had them erect an oblong-shaped house with only one entrance. Then he stretched a mat over the hole, and seated his subjects all around the edges to hold it taut. This done, he sent for his son, whose death he was seeking.

As the boy drew near the entrance, his father, from within the house, called to him to enter. Suspicious, Lahi thrust his spear through the mat and discovered the treachery. So, quickly closing the door, he set fire to the house, and destroyed his treacherous father and all his faithless subjects. Then Lahi became king.

The Small Wise Boy and The Little Fool

A Legend of Kauai

There were two brothers who lived on the flats at Nukole, between Hanamaulu and the Waila stream. Their names were Waa-waa-iki-naau-ao, The-Wise-One, and Waa-waa-iki-naaupo, The-Stupid-One.

One day they decided to go to Waialeale, to exploit their bird preserves. In those days, each person had his special bird grounds as well as fishing grounds. No one could trespass on their rights. As they were starting out, The-Wise-One said to The-Stupid-One. "When we catch the birds, every bird that has two holes in its beak belongs to me. That is my mark. Those that have only one hole belong to you."

So every bird that The-Stupid-One caught, he gave to his brother, for they all had two holes in their beaks. He would say, "This is yours, it bas your mark." So, when they started home, The-Wise-One had all the birds, and The-Stupid-One had none.

Then The Stupid-One went crying to his mother, saying, "All the birds we caught today belong to my brother. They had his mark. I had none to bring home."

After he had explained to his mother about the marks, she comforted him in these words, "That is all right. We will fix it so that you get all the birds next time."

Then she got a lot of breadfruit gum, and told The-Stupid-One to take it with him. When he caught a bird, he must pull all the feathers off before he gave it to his brother. Then when they were ready to start home, he would have a big pile of feathers. He must let The Wise-One go first, with the pack of birds. Then The-Stupid-One must smear the gum all over himself, and roll in the feathers. They would stick to him, and he would be completely covered. Then he must follow his brother very quietly, until they got to the path that crosses the top of the hill, Ka-ili-hina-lea. When he reached this spot, The-Stupid-One must rush up behind his brother, crying in a loud voice, "*Apau!* The *akua* of the mountain is after you! He will grab you!"

The mother continued in these words, "Then your brother will look back and see you, and be frightened. He will drop the birds, and run. Then you can pick up the birds and bring them home. You will have them all, and you will have only a little way to carry them."

The-Stupid-One carried out his mother's instructions. All happened as she had said. So that time The-Stupid-One had the best of it in the end.

Another time the two boys went fishing. The-Wise-One told The Stupid-One that all the fish with two eyes belonged to him. All the fish with one eye, The-Stupid-One could have. The-Stupid-One gave all the fish he caught to his brother, as they had his mark. So The-Wise-One had a big pile of fish. But at last The-Stupid-One caught a fish from the deep sea that had only one eye. So he had something to take home.

KAMAPUAA

A Legend of Kauai

KAMAPUAA CAME TO KIPUKAI, ON the southeast coast of Kauai, in the form of a large fish called by the Hawaiians *humuhumu-a-puaa*. This is a black fish, with a long snout like that of a hog. As soon as Kamapuaa had landed at Point Kipu-iki he changed himself into a hog, and rooted in the sand to get a drink of water. At low tide fresh water is still to be found at Point Kipu-iki.

After Kamapuaa had rested a while, he tried to climb a small, steep cliff nearby, but was unable to do so. When darkness hid him, he ate all the sweet potatoes and sugar cane belonging to the natives. Then he crossed over to a big rock on the side of the hill to the west, and lay down to sleep.

When the natives wakened in the morning, they found their sugar cane and potatoes gone. Seeing in the fields the tracks of a large hog, they followed them with their dogs until they came upon the hog, fast asleep. They quickly tied his feet together with strong ropes. He was so large that twenty men had to carry him to the village, where they prepared an *imu* in which to cook him.

When the *imu* was red hot, the men brought a rope to strangle their victim. Then the hog stretched himself, breaking the ropes, and walked away as a man. The men were so astonished that they did not dare to follow. Even in the form of a man, Kamapuaa retained something of the hog. Although his face was very handsome, he still had stiff black bristles down his back. However, he always wore a cape to cover the bristles.

Kamapuaa went on until he came to the hidden spring of Kemamo, over which two *kupua* kept watch. Being thirsty, the stranger asked for water. When the *kupua* refused to give him any, he turned himself into a hog again, and rooted in the earth until he found a spring. Then he seized the *kupua* and threw them across the valley, where they were turned into two large rocks, which can be seen to this day. The water of this spring was very famous for its sparkle, and in the old days, it was taken in gourds to the other islands for special occasions.

Later, Kamapuaa found another spring, in which he lay down and went to sleep. The water of this spring is still so bitter that no animal will drink it, and it is still called Wai-a-ka-puaa, the Water-of-the-Pig. While Kamapuaa was sleeping, the giant Limaloa, Long-Arm, from Kekaha, saw the huge creature lying in the mud, and so he put his back to a large boulder to roll it down on the hog and crush him. As the stone came near, Kamapuaa awoke and threw a small stone under it, which wedged the great boulder on the hillside, so that it did not fall on him. These stones can still be pointed out on the Kipukai trail.

Then Limaloa saw that the object he was trying to kill was a man. He made friends with Kamapuaa, and told him that on the other side of the ridge, there were two beautiful women, whom he had been courting. They had rejected his suit, but since Kamapuaa was so much more handsome, he might be successful should he attempt his fortune.

The two men crossed from Kipukai, over the gap of Kemamo. As they were coming down the hill on the Lihue side, Kamapuaa slid on a big rock; the groove that his hoof made, can still be seen. The friends saw the two beautiful sisters washing their faces and combing their hair at the two clear pools, like basins, called Ka-wai-o-ka-pakilokilo, the Waters where-the-Image-is-Reflected. The pools were in a large rock on the hill side and can still be seen at the left of where the paved trail begins Kamapuaa slid down the slope, and, standing where his reflection could be seen, began to sing.

The sisters were greatly impressed by the beautiful reflection in the water. They looked up, and seeing the handsome stranger, they fell in love with him at first sight, and invited him to go home with them. Kamapuaa said that he would go with them, if his *akua* could accompany him. To this the sisters gladly consented. But when they saw the rejected Limala, they cried, "That man is no *akua*. He is the one who has been annoying us by his attentions and presents. We do not care for him."

However, Kamapuaa would not go without his newfound friend. So, in order to have the handsome stranger, the sisters allowed Limaloa to follow to the home of their brother, who was king of the Puna side of Kanai. This stretched from Kipukai to Anahola. The king soon gave his sisters to Kamapuaa in marriage.

At this time the Puna side was engaged in a battle with the Kona side, which included all the country from Koloa to Mana. Kamapuaa would wait in the house until all the men had gone to the battlefield. Then after having made all his body invisible, except his hands, which held a club, he would follow the Puna men to battle, and strike the Kona chiefs on the head. From the dead chiefs he would take their feather capes and helmets. Then he would return home as a hog, and dirty the floormats. When the two beautiful sisters had gone down to the stream to wash the mats the hog had befouled, Kamapuaa would hide the capes and helmets under the *punee*, or beds, which were made with frameworks of *lau-hala* logs, covered with many finely woven mats. Gradually the *punee* grew higher and higher, for he continued stealing and hiding the capes and helmets for days, until he had collected a huge store of them.

The king began to miss these things, which were always his perquisites from the booty taken. But he was unable to find who was stealing them, or where they were hidden. Finally he called his *kahuna* to help him find the guilty person. The *kahuna* told the king to build a platform, and then to summon all his people, for it was known that the hand which had killed so many chiefs had one day been wounded on the thumb by a spear. The king would stand on the platform, and order everyone to raise his hands. Then he could easily see the wounded hand, and so find the thief.

The king followed out the instructions of his *kahuna*. At a given signal all hands were raised. There was no wounded hand to be seen. Then the king was told that his brother-in-law, Kamapuaa, was not there. So his house was searched, and he was found. Behold, his hand was wounded!

Upon further search, the feather capes and helmets were found. The king was very angry. He gave Kamapuaa his choice of either leaving his home, or being put to death. Kamapuaa wisely chose the former punishment. He next went to Oahu, then to Maui, and Hawaii, where he had many adventures, but he never returned to Kauai. Limaloa returned to Kekaha, where, it is said, that, to this day, at dawn at certain times of the year, he can be seen at Kaunalewa, near Waiawa. Dressed in a yellow feather cloak and helmet he comes out of the phantom houses, which can be dimly seen near the coconut trees, and strides along with his spear.

WILLIAM HYDE RICE

KAWELO OF KAUAI

K awelo, the Waving-of-the-Flag, the great opponent of Kauahon, the giant of Hanalei, was the son of Maihuna and Malaiakalani. He was born in Hanamaulu, Kauai. He had two older brothers, one older sister, and one younger brother, Kamalama. Kawelo was such a good son that he was known as Kawelo-Lei-Makua, Kawelo-Who-Cherished-His-Parents.

The maternal grandparents of Kawelo were celebrated for their skill in phrenology. So when still a small boy Kawelo was taken by his parents to them, and they foretold that he would be a good soldier, a strong man, a conqueror, a son who would bring life to their bones.

Wishing to care tenderly for such a grandson, his grandparents took him to live with them at Wailua, where lived Aikanaka, the young prince, and Kauahoa, boys of the same age as Kawelo, with whom he played.

Kawelo developed a great appetite. He would eat the contents of an *imu*, or oven, of food at one time. His grandparents grew weary of trying to satisfy this huge appetite, and so they tried to divert the boy's mind. They gave him a canoe to paddle up and down the Wailua River.

As soon as Kauahoa saw Kawelo enjoying his canoe, he made a kite and flew it. At once Kawelo asked his grandparents to make him a kite. So the two boys flew their kites together until one day Kawelo's caught in the string of his friend's and broke it, freeing the kite, which flew off and lit at a place above Koloa, still called Hooleinapea, the Fall-of-the-Kite. The ridge still shows the dent where the kite struck it.

Kawelo feared that Kauahoa would be angry and punish him, as Kaushoa was the larger of the two, but Kauahoa said nothing about the kite, and Kawelo decided that the young giant was afraid of him.

Aikanaka, Man-Eater,[3] the prince, ruled over his two friends even as boys. Whatever he asked them to do they did. So they grew to manhood.

In the meantime the older brothers of Kawelo went to Oahu, where Kakuhihewa was ruling. This king had among his retainers a very strong man, the strongest wrestler in the islands. The boys very often went surfboard-riding, and when this exericse was over, they would wrestle with the great champion.

---

3. *Aikanaka* is used figuratively. The Hawaiians were not cannibals.

HAWAIIAN LEGENDS   61

After these boys had been away some years, their grandparents had a great desire to see them, so taking Kawelo with them the old people paddled to Oahu and landed at Waikiki.

On Oahu Kawelo met and soon married Kanewahineikiacha and in order to provide food for himself and his wife he worked everyday in the taro patch.

One day as he was at work he heard great shouting down by the sea. His grandparents told him that his brothers were wrestling with the king's strong man. When one of them was thrown down the people shouted.

At once Kawelo longed to see the sport, but his grandparents forbade his going. So he waited until they were away and then he hurried to the sea, where he saw his brothers surfing. He borrowed a surfboard and joined his brothers and later followed them to the wrestling place. When he stood up to wrestle with the strong man, his brothers tried to prevent him by saying that he was too young, that he was not strong enough. Kawelo did not listen to them and to everyone's surprise he threw the king's great wrestler. This angered the brothers, who were ashamed of their lack of strength, and so they hurried to their grandparents, and told them that Kawelo had been throwing stones at them. Receiving little sympathy they decided to return to Kauai.

Then Kawelo began to desire other accomplishments. First he longed to be able to hula, which meant a training in an art far more diversified than mere dancing. After long schooling the pupils had to pass a strict examination before they could appear in public. But this graceful and difficult art Kawelo could not master, so he turned his mind to other things. His father-in-law taught him, and his wife as well, all manner of spear throwing. Next he wanted to learn to fish well. Makuakeke, the celebrated fisherman, became his teacher.

At dawn Kawelo awakened his teacher with these words, "Makuakeke, awake! The sun is high. Bring the fishhooks and the nets. Let us fish."

So the fisherman prepared everything. They got into a canoe and out, paddled out to deep water. As they were going, the older man called "Kawelo, the lei of his parents, my king fisherman of Kauai, we will fish here."

But Kawelo answered, "Not here. We shall go on until we reach the point of Kaena. Hold on to the canoe."

Then with one mighty stroke of the paddle the canoe lay off Honolulu harbor, with two strokes it neared Puuloa, and with three it reached Waianae. There Kawelo chewed some *kukui* nuts and blew the oil over the sea so that the water became calm and they could see the bottom. The canoe drifted from the shallow water into the deep as the men fished for ulua.

As it grew late Makuakeke urged Kawelo to return home, for he knew that it was time for Uhumakaikai, the fish god, to appear and he greatly feared this fish.

So the tired fishermen went home. After Kawelo had bathed, he ordered his steward to bring him his evening meal. Forty calabashes of poi, and forty *laulau*, or bundles (of pig) wrapped in ti leaves and cooked in an underground *imu*, or oven, were set before him, but this was so enough to satisfy his huge appetite. The same amount was set before the second time, and having eaten it he lay down to sleep.

As the sun was setting. Kawelo awoke and ordered the mats to be spread, and the pillows and bed tapas to be prepared. Before retiring he read the signs of the heavens and learned that Haupu and Kalanips, two mountain peaks near Nawiliwili Bay, were being burned up. "Alas!" he cried, "My love for my parents is coming to me. They may be in trouble I fear that they are being killed."

His wife, who did not know that her husband was able to read the heavens, asked, "How are you able to go to Kauai and back so soon?"

Kawelo answered, "If your parents were in trouble you would weep. Your tears would flow. You care not for my beloved ones."

Early the next morning Kawelo called the fisherman and paddled out to their fishing waters. Soon Makuakeke saw the storm clouds gathering in the sky and knew that the fish god was coming. As the huge fish swam towards them Kawelo threw his net and caught him. Then the fish, pulling the canoe with him, swam out to sea until the men could no longer see their homes or the surf beating on the shore. They went so rapidly that they soon came to Kauai, where the fish turned and swam back with them to Waikiki. There at last the men were able to kill him.

As Kawelo jumped ashore, he saw two messengers from Kauai standing near his six soldiers, who were very skilled in throwing the spear. Kawelo noticed that these soldiers were drawing their spears, and he heard one of the messengers cry, "They are trying to spear Kawelo before he is ready. If they do, our journey to Oahu will have been in vain."

Kamalama, Kawelo's younger brother, answered, "Watch. You will see that the spears thrown at him will be like water."

First two of the soldiers threw their spears in vain at Kawelo. When they were weary, two others, more skilled, took their turns, and so on until all had tried. But this was only a game to Kawelo.

Then Kamalama was told by his brother to bring the sharp spears with which they could do battle. Taking the celebrated spears he cried, "Kawelo, keep your eyes wide open. If you wink your eyes once I will spear you."

Bracing himself, he threw the spear at Kawelo with all his might. Kawelo dodged it, and it flew on until it came to the surf at Waikiki, so great had been the force which sent it. Then Kamalama was told to throw the second spear directly at the stomach of his brother. Again Kawelo dodged it and this time it flew beyond the surf.

When the messengers from Kauai had seen Kawelo's skill in dodging spears, they marvelled at his strength and declared that he would be the conqueror of the islands. After so much exercise Kawelo hurried to his bath and then sat down to eat his forty calabashes of poi and forty *laulau* of pig. As before, his hunger was not satisfied until he had been served the same amount again. Then, calling the messengers to him, he inquired what had brought them from Kauai.

They answered, "Kawelo, we have come to take you home to your parents, who are in sore need. They have been driven from their homes and have nothing to eat. You must return to fight with Aikanaka, the cruel prince."

Without replying to them, Kawelo ordered his wife to secure from her father spears, bows and arrows used for shooting rats, and the ax that he used for hewing out canoes. All these things he would need on Kauai.

After his wife had crossed the stream and walked beyond the coconut trees, Kawelo told Kamalama to follow her, concealed, and to listen to the words of her father.

When Kanewahine came to her father's house she found that he had gone to prepare and for the gods. Now the building where he was working was *kapu* for women, so the mother approached as near as she dared and then wailed loudly to attract his attention. Ceasing his prayers to the gods, the father hurried to his daughter, and asked, "What great thing has brought you here? Are you not afraid of the *akau* which hover about?"

Kanewahine answered, "I came to get the spears, the bows and arrows, and the ax for my husband who must go to Kauai to do battle."

Her father began to berate his son-in-law in these words: "Your husband is a plover with small feet. He is a bird that runs along the beach and is overthrown by the beating surf. He is like a banana tree without strength; he is like a *puhala* tree growing with its roots out of the ground. He is not strong like me, your father, large from head to feet, whom neither the Kona storms nor the wind from the mountains can harm."

"Be careful how you speak of my husband," warned Kanewahine. "He will know whatever you say."

"What wonderful ears he must have!" jeered the angry father. "He is on the Kona side and we are at Koolau."

His daughter replied, "My husband's powerful god, Kalanikilo, has heard your words and he will tell. My husband knows everything. Nothing is hidden from him."

"If that is the case," said her father, "someone must be listening who will carry my words to him. Come, my sons, and we will find the guilty one."

And so they searched everywhere but no one was to be found, for as soon as Kamalama had seen them coming he had hurried to tell Kawelo all he had heard. When he began his story his brother stopped him, saying that he knew all. This made Kamalama very angry and he cried, "If you have such good ears why did you send me to that place where I have no friends? I wish to eat."

The head steward carried out forty sweet potatoes and forty *laulau* of pig. While they were eating, the father-in-law with his sons arrived and Kawelo told him all he had said.

"See! It is as I said," cried Kanewahine, "his god is very powerful."

"Yes," answered the father, "I see that your husband can hear in Kona what has been said in Koolau."

Then Kawelo, anxious to punish his father-in-law, said that they must try spear throwing. His father-in-law told one of his sons to try first, but Kawelo would not hear of this. "The teacher must first try with the scholar," he said. "Then it will be seen which one is stronger."

So the man and his sons were on one side against Kawelo. His father-in-law threw the first spear which was warded off, and flying back, hit the thrower, knocking him down. As his father-in-law rolled over in the sand, Kawelo cried, "My spear, Kuikaa, is stronger than yours. It has hit your jaw. You are being punished for what you said of me. A rooster fed in the sun is stronger than one fed in the shade. One kick from the rooster fed in the sun will knock you down."

Seeing her father lying on the sand, Kanewahine ran to him and, pouring water on his head, restored him to consciousness.

After this trial of spears, Kawelo sent his brother and his wife with two soldiers to Punloa to beg a canoe from Kakuhihewa, the king of Oahu. When they came before the king, Kanewahine stated their mission. The king gladly gave them a large double canoe because he feared Kawelo and was glad to hear that he was leaving for Kauai to do battle with Aikanaka.

So they returned to Waikiki in the canoe and Kawelo began his prepa rations for leaving. As soon as all was ready they set sail and went ashore at Waianae where they built a heian to Kawelo's gods. After Kawelo had placed his gods in this heiau he asked advice from them, for he was uncertain in his mind about this journey. The feathers on one god, Kane-i-ka-pualena, the Yellow-Feathered-God, stood straight up, showing that he was not afraid of the task before them. The other god, Kalanihehu, the Scatterer-of-the-Heavens, gave no sign. But Kawelo believed he had seen a propitious omen and at evening he left Oahu.

Before morning Kawelo saw Keaolewa, the clouds on the top of Haupu, floating towards them like a great white bird. Soon Kalanipuu came into sight.

These sights were not visible to the other passengers of the cance and Kawelo's uncle exclaimed, "You must be telling us falsely. We have often been on this voyage with your parents, but always one night and half a day passed before we could see Keaolewa flying towards us like a bird. You say you see it before dawn."

But at daybreak all were able to see that Kawelo was speaking truth fully and in a short time the canoe lay off Hanamaulu, where the messengers urged Kawelo to land so that he could see his parents and friends before going to battle with Aikanaka. Kawelo refused to do this and ordered Kamalama to turn the canoe towards Wailua.

As the canoe anchored at Wailua, Kawelo told his brother to feed all the men so that they would be strong for the work before them.

The people on Nounou saw the canoe, and Aikanaka sent his messengers to find out what sort of canoe it might be, friendly or warlike. If friendly, the passengers were to be given food, tapas, and shelter. If warlike, the two great generals of Aikanaka were to give battle at once.

In the meantime Kawelo, wrapped in mats, had been placed on the *pola*, the platform joining the double canoes, where he was covered with

WILLIAM HYDE RICE

coconut leaves. When Kamalama saw the messengers swimming out to them, he called to Kawelo, "A man from our king is coming. He is swimming towards us."

As the messenger climbed aboard he asked, "Why have these canoes come?"

"To give battle," answered Kamalama, boldly.

"Who is the general?" inquired the man.

"I," said Kamalama.

"Where is Kawelo?"

"He is on Oahu."

"What is that bundle on the *pola*?"

"That is our food and clothing for this trip."

The messenger, a little suspicious, stepped on the bundle, but, as it did not move, he was deceived.

Then Kamalama asked how the king wished to give battle. He was told to go ashore where, after they had rested, eaten, and put on their war *malo*, they could begin the battle.

"But," warned the messenger, "you cannot win. We feared only Kawelo. Since he is not here you cannot hope for victory. You would do well to return to Oahu. This is not a canoe fit for doing battle with Kauai, Such a canoe must needs be a big canoe, a long canoe, and a wide canoe."

During this conversation crowds of people had gathered on the beach with the two head warriors. Each warrior had four hundred soldiers not to mention the women and children-all clamoring to begin the fight at once.

But the messenger, mindful of his promise to Kamalama, ordered them back while some of his men carried the enemy's canoe up on the dry sand.

While this was going on Kawelo had secretly told his brother to loosen the rope that bound his feet. This done, he stood up with his mighty spear, Kuikaa, the Whizzing-Point, in his hand. Seeing him, his followers cried out, "Kawelo is on the canoe!"

The word Kawelo aroused such great fear in the hearts of the men who were carrying the canoe that they dropped it, killing several. At once the soldiers of Aikanaka surrounded the canoe.

Kawelo thrust his spear on the right side of the canoe and killed a great number. Then he turned to the left and killed many more. As soon as the Kauai soldiers saw how great the slaughter was, they retreated to the hill of Nounou. There they met great numbers of men hurrying to re enforce their friends by the sea.

After the retreat Kawelo ordered his brother to push the canoe back into the sea where he could watch the battle. Then Kamalama arranged the soldiers skillfully as he had been directed. Kawelo's adopted child, Kauluiki, Little-Rolling-Stone, led the right wing, and another adopted child, Kalaumeki, Meki-Leaf, led the left.

Seeing that Kawelo was not on land the soldiers of Kauai came forward again, and engaged in furious strife. Kamalama was in the thickest of the battle, fighting with great courage. Kauluiki retreated to the shore, but Kalaumeki kept on fighting, killing many.

When Kawelo saw how things were going, he called out in a loud voice, "When we conquer the island, Kamalama shall have all the Kona side of Kauai and Kalaumeki shall have all the Koolau side."

Hearing these words, Kauluiki grieved deeply because he had retreated. "It would have been better to have stayed on Oahu," he mourned. "There I at least had taro to eat. Here I have nothing."

When the messenger saw that the generals and best soldiers of his king had been killed he hurried to carry this news to Aikanaka. Kawelo asked Kamalama to follow the messenger and when he overtook him to scratch him with his spear, to mark him, but to let him go on his errand. Kamalama overtook the messenger before he was halfway up the hill. Tearing off his clothes, he beat him and then let him go. As the poor man ran to his king he cried, "We have no men left. All are killed. When I swam out to the canoe, Kamalama was the leader. Kawelo was nowhere to be seen. When the canoe came ashore, Kawelo appeared."

This news was a great surprise to Aikanaka because when he had heard that messengers had been sent to Oahu for Kawelo he had called together his bravest and most valiant warriors. Kauahoa had also been ordered to join them on the hill of Nounou, which had been well fortified. There provisions had been stored. The hill teemed with the celebrated soldiers of Kauai.

As the king was listening to the report of his messenger, two of his head soldiers, Kaihupepe, Flat-Nose, and Mano, Shark, asked if they could go down to the sea with eight hundred soldiers and engage in battle with the invaders. They asked only for the king's messenger as guide. The king granted this request and they advanced to join in battle.

The fresh troops met Kamalama's men and were slaughtered. Only the messenger escaped. He hurried to carry the news of this disaster to

WILLIAM HYDE RICE

his king. "That is not a battle yonder," he cried, "it is a fire. Kamalama can throw his spear through ten men."

Great anger filled the heart of Aikanaka. Two other generals boasted of their strength and begged to be allowed to fight with their four hundred soldiers. As they advanced, Kamalama met them. In the battle which followed the men from Oahu showed their wonderful skill in spear throwing. They could spear an ant or a fly. Easily they killed all but the two generals. Then the hand of one of these men was speared.

But this battle had been so furious that Kamalama and Kalaumeki were beginning to be weary, and they were being hard pressed by the enemy. Kawelo saw this and called to them to retreat. While they were retreating, Kawelo ordered his paddlers to paddle the canoe to the shore. There he learned that most of the Kauai soldiers had been killed. The rest were about to retreat.

Kawelo then angered his brother by granting more land to his stepson. Kamalama left the battlefield, but was brought back by these flattering words, "Why do you depart, my young brother? You are the greatest soldier of all. You are hungry now; so your strength is waning."

Just then reinforcements came from Nounou and the Oahu soldiers retreated to the spot where Kawelo was standing. Seeing Walaheeikio, one of Kauai's most celebrated soldiers, advancing, Kawelo thus addressed him, "If you will join my forces, I will give you my sister as your wife."

This promise made the warrior think that Kawelo feared him. So he replied, "It is not for you to give me a wife. I shall kill you, and Aikanala will offer your body as a sacrifice to his gods, I and my men will eat cooked taro on Kauai."

This vain boasting amused Kawelo, who warned, "Break the point off your spear before you thrust it at Kawelo."

"I will not have to break my spear to strike you," laughed the soldier. "You are as large as the end of a house. I must be an awkward animal if I miss you."

"You cannot hit a flying flag," ridiculed Kawelo. "You might hit my waving *malo*. Your shameful boasting will make you weep."

The two warriors raised their spears at the same time and threw them. Kawelo dodged the spear which just touched his *malo* and passed on into the ground. With shame, Walaheeikio turned to hasten back to Nounou but Kawelo threw his spear at his back and killed him.

So only Maomaoikio was left. Pity for the lone warrior filled Kawelo's heart and he offered him a wife if he would desert Aikanaka. But this soldier answered as his companion had answered, and threw his spear at Kawelo. Kawelo dodged it and threw his mighty spear at the king's faithful soldier. Then his canoe was left to drift without its paddler.

The messenger ran to Nounou and reported to Aikanaka, the boasting of his generals and their death at the hands of Kawelo. Then the king cried, "Now a cold chill numbs my bones. The house that gave us shelter is broken."

A soldier, Kahakaloa, skilled in throwing and dodging spears cheered the broken king with these words, "When did Kawelo learn to fight? We all lived here together and he was no more skilled than others. He has not been on Oahu very long. How can he be so skilled even though his father-in-law has been teaching him? I have fought with his father-in-law and neither could win from the other. How then can Kawelo defeat me? So, O King, give me five forties of men and I shall join battle with Kawelo and his younger brother."

Permission was gladly given by the king and Kahakaloa advanced to the foot of Nounou where he met Kamalama. In the battle which ensued, his strength and valor were shown, for he pressed his rival back to the spot where Kawelo was standing. There Kawelo angered him by calling him names, "*Lae-paa*! Branded, son of a slave! *Ai-opala*, eater of rubbish! Dog! *Ai-hemu*, eater of leavings!" This was a great insult to a high chief of Kauai.

At length the two warriors stood ready for the encounter. Their spears were thrown at the same time. Kawelo was struck and stunned and his body rolled in the dust. Kahakaloa lost one ear and a little finger.

The king's messenger urged the soldier to strike the fallen Kawelo again, as his eyes were still open, but Kahakaloa answered, "He is killed by one blow from a young man. I shall not strike him again or he will go down to Milu and boast that I had to strike him twice. Now let us go home to eat. After that we shall return and finish our enemy."

Kamalama ran to his brother, for he believed that he had been killed. But in a short time Kawelo sat up. His dizziness left him. He asked where his antagonist had gone. Then he strengthened himself with food.

Kahakaloa, in the meantime, had hurried to his king, where he boasted that he had killed the mighty Kawelo, and that he would soon go back to the sea to put out his light forever. Hearing that his great rival was no more. Aikanaka ordered his steward to place the choicest food before the valiant soldier and the faithful messenger.

While this was being prepared, the king noticed that Kahakaloa had lost a finger and he inquired how the accident had happened.

"That was a branch on the outside which was easily struck," answered the soldier.

"And how about your ear?"

"Oh, that was a branch on top also easily cut off," replied the wounded man.

After Kahakaloa had eaten the food from the calabash he placed the empty vessel on his head as a helmet and went forth to destroy his rival.

Seeing someone coming, Kamalama called to his brother, "A bald headed man is advancing. I can see the sun shining on his forehead."

But Kawelo was not deceived. He recognized his former antagonist and planned revenge. As Kahakaloa came before him, Kawelo struck the calabash on his head. Being broken, it fell over his eyes so that he could not see, and he was easily killed.

Again the messenger had to carry news of defeat to his king, whose only comment was, "How could he live, so wounded? He was only Kawelo's pig."

There still remained on Nounou, Kauahoa, the strongest of all the king's soldiers. He was known all over the islands for his size. He it was whom Kawelo feared most of all. However, Kawelo remembered their boyhood days when he had broken his friend's kite and had escaped unpunished. If Kauahoa feared him as a boy, possibly he still did. This thought cheered him and he planned how he could gain a victory over his old-time opponent.

Now when Kauahoa heard that Kahakaloa had fallen in the dust, he vowed to seek revenge with his spear, a whole koa tree from Kahihikolo, above Kilanea, so large that the birds sang in its branches while it was being carried. The giant stripped some of the branches from this tree, and they are growing at Kahihikolo now.

As this giant with his huge spear came down from Nounou he was so large that he hid the sun. A cold chill mumbed the bones of Kawelo. Fear filled his brave heart. But he prepared for battle.

On his right he placed his wife with her *pikoi*. On his left he stationed Kamalama. Behind him he ordered his foster sons to wait. Thus Kawelo stood with his mighty spear, ten fathoms long.

Kawelo knew that by skill only could he hope for victory. He decided not to wait long. Then he called out:

> *I remember the days when we were young.*
> *Swelled now is the* **limu** *of Hanalei.*
> *Swelled above the eyes is the cloud of morning.*
> *In vain is the battle at the hands of children.*
> *The great battle will follow,*
> *As the deep sea follows the shallow water.*
> *In vain are the clouds dispersed.*
> *O Kauahoa, the strong one of Kualoa!*
> *Awake, O Kamalama, the strong one of Kualoa!*
> *Awake, Kawelo, the strong one of Waikiki!*
> *Awake, Kaelehapuna, the strong one of Waimea!*
> *We will all gather together at noonday.*
> *Postpone the battle, my brother. Leave me.*
> *This is not the day for us to give an exhibition of battle,*
> *At Waikaee for our lord and older brothers.*
> *Awake, O Hanalei, the land of chill and rain,*
> *The land where the clouds hover!*
> *Awake O Kauahoa, the handsome one of Hanalei!*

To these words the giant of Hanalei answered, "Today we will give battle. Today either my spear will seek your death or your spear will seek mine. Today on one of us must fall the heavy sickness."

This answer alarmed Kawelo, but he fanned his flickering courage with the remembrance of the kite incident and replied:

> *Hanalei, the land of cold and wet,*
> *Hanalei, the land where the clouds hover!*
> *The Ukiukiu, the northerly storm, of Hanakoa,*
> *The cliffs of Kalehuawehi are in vain.*
> *The* **lama** *and* **wiliwili** *are in flower.*
> *The rain that flies beyond Manalahoa*
> *Is like Kauahoa, the man that Kamalama will defeat.*

Having spoken thus, Kawelo said to his wife, "Throw your pikoi high as the ridge pole of Kauai is high. If we kill this giant, Kauai is ours. We shall cover ourselves with the fine mats of Niihau, and shall eat of the birds of Kaula."

Placing his brother and his foster children behind him, Kawelo at last was ready. Then, as Kauahoa threw his spear, Kawelo's wife caught it and drew it to one side with her *pikoi*, enabling her husband to dodge it As the giant stooped down to pick up his spear, Kawelo cut him in two. So died the last of the strong men of Aikanaka.

That night Kawelo said to his wife, "I and my brother will go up to the bill of Nounou. If you see a fire burning you will know that we have conquered Kauai."

Ascending Nounou, Kawelo called out, "Aikanaka, let us be friends. Let us sleep together on the mats of Niihau."

The king did not reply. His men told him that Kawelo was tired and would soon be asleep. But they heard Kawelo asking if there were no men left on Kauai.

Aikanaka answered that only twelve soldiers were left. Then he begged his *kahuna* to let him go and meet Kawelo. They replied that a king could not fight with a servant whose duty it was to count cockroaches.

Kawelo heard these words, which filled him with such shame that he started to roll down the hill. His wife threw her *pikoi* and kept him back, saying, "Why should you be ashamed? If you are really a slave, kill yourself. If you had been a slave, you would have been killed during this battle. The roosters are kings because they sleep on the top of the house. They waken you in the morning."

The *kahuna* told Aikanaka to answer that roosters were slaves.

"Oh, no," replied Kawelo, "you use the feathers of roosters to make kahili to wave over your kings."

Suddenly, a stillness fell on Nounou. Aikanaka and his men had fled to Hanapepe. Then Kawelo built a big fire on the hill. Seeing this, his brother and sons knew that Kauai belonged to him and so they hurried to the hill. There Kawelo divided the island, giving Koolau to Kalaumeki, Puna to Kaeleha, and Kona to Kamalama. The whole island was under the supervision of Kawelo, who lived in peace with his parents at Hanamaulu.

Aikanaka was living at Hanapepe with no honor, no food, no tapa. With his own hands he had to cultivate the taro patches. After he had been living in this manner for sometime, Kaeleha left Kapaa and came to Hanapepe. There he met Aikanaka, who gave him food. A friendship grew between them and the former king gave his daughter in marriage to his conqueror's foster son.

As time went on Kaeleha grieved because he had nothing to give in return for so much kindness. At last his shame was so great that he decided to lessen it by telling Aikanaka that he could conquer Kaweln by throwing stones at him. This secret brought gladness to the king's heart and he cried, "My bones shall live again!" So Aikanaka and Kaeleha counseled together. The king sent his men to pile up stones near Wahiawa.

In the meantime these plans had been carried to Kawelo, who sent to find out from Kamalama if they were true. Kamalama hurried to Wahiawa, where he saw a great many people on the plains gathering and piling up stones. While he watched, a man approached him and said that these stones were being gathered to give battle to Kawelo, the usurper.

Kamalama sent this report to Kawelo, who was filled with anger. He hastened to Wahiawa, where he discovered Kaeleha's war canoes concealed behind the great pile of stones. There, too, he saw many men armed with stones, ready to give battle. Kawelo had only his spear and his wife's *pikoi*. He and his wife had to fight with all of Aikanaka's men. It was impossible for the valiant Kawelo to dodge all the stones which were flying at him from all directions. They piled up over his head. Several times he shook them off. At last he became weak and the stones were as a grave to him. His wife, wailing loudly, fled.

Believing that he was dead, the men removed the stones and beat his bruised body with sticks until they could feel no more pulse. Then messengers were sent to proclaim Aikanaka king of Kauai again.

Men carried the body of Kawelo to Koloa, where Aikanaka had built a heiau. There they laid the body and covered it with banana leaves, planning to return in the morning to offer the sacrifice.

The heat created by the banana leaves brought warmth to the cold body, and at midnight Kawelo returned to life. He got slowly to his feet and walked about the enclosure waiting for daylight.

The guard heard the footsteps in the heiau and fear took hold of him, for he believed that Kawelo's ghost had returned to seek vengeance. Creeping up to the wall he saw Kawelo standing and so he called, "Is that in truth you, Kawelo? Has death departed from you?"

A voice answered, "Where is Aikanaka with his men? Where am

I?" When he heard these words, the guard knew that Kawelo was not dead.

"They are far distant," replied the guard. "They are sleeping. At sunrise they return to place your body on the altar and to offer you as a sacrifice to Aikanaka's god. It is wonderful that you live. I will help you in any way I can, even if in so doing, death come to my bones."

These words cheered Kawelo and he asked for his mighty spear. Then he directed the guard in these words, "Towards morning I shall lie down. You cover me again with the banana leaves. When Aikanaka and his friends enter the heiau whisper to me."

So Kawelo lay concealed under the banana leaves. Aikanaka did not come until noon and the hidden man was greatly annoyed as he was very uncomfortable.

At last he heard the guard whisper, "Kawelo, Kawelo, awake! Aikanaka, your treacherous son, and all their soldiers are in the heiau!" Then pulling off the banana leaves the guard called aloud as Kawelo stood up, "Behold! Kawelo has come to life!" Utter astonishment seized the men. They could not believe that this was he whom they had left as dead.

Stepping towards Kaeleha, Kawelo cried, "My son whom I fed and cared for, why did you turn against me? Today you shall pay the cost. And you, Aikanaka, shall die today, too."

Then Kawelo hurled his faithful spear and killed all but the guard. To him he gave Koloa, where he should reign as high chief.

Kawela returned to Hanamaulu and there lived in peace until the day of his death.

THE DESTRUCTION OF THE AKUA ON NIHAU

The people of the islands of Kauai and Niihau were accustomed to going to one end of Niihau to fish. But it often happened that while they were sleeping on the sand after a hard day's fishing, the *akua* would come and devour many of the men.

At last one brave man declared that he would destroy the *akua* and rid the island of this danger. So he built a long house, similar to a canoe house, leaving only one entrance. Then he made many *kii*, or wooden images of people, placing in the heads mottled gray and black eyes of *opihi*, or mussel shell. These images he put in the house, concealing himself outside.

At night the *akua* began to come for their usual meal. Looking into the house they saw the *kii* with their shining eyes. At first this surprised them, but as the images lay very still, the *akua* decided that the Kauai men slept with their eyes open, and so they entered and tried to eat the images, with dire results. Their teeth were caught in the wood, and while they were struggling to free them, the crafty Kauai man quickly shut the door and set fire to the house, and all the cruel akua were burned to death.

Thereafter Niihau became safe for fishermen, and this part of the island still bears the name Kii.

Pakaa and His Son Ku-a-Pakaa

Ku-a-nuuanu was the head steward of Keawe-nui-a-umi, the Great-One-in-Umi's-Presence, son of Umi, king of Hawaii, and god of all the winds, which he kept in a huge calabash. The king loved his steward greatly and placed great confidence in everything he did.

One day the desire to visit the other islands of the group came to Ku-a-nu'uanu, and so as he waited on his king he said to him, "My Lord the King, if you have any love in your heart for me you will allow me to visit the other islands. You will not miss me, for you have many servants. If you need me at anytime send a messenger and I shall gladly return."

When the king had heard these words he was very sad at heart for his steward was very skilled in serving him. Nevertheless, he gave his permission and bade his servant farewell, with these words, "Aloha. May the spirits of our ancestors keep you until we meet again."

Ku-a-nu'uanu prepared his tapa and *malo* for the journey. Then getting into his canoe, he paddled well and soon came to Lahaina, where he went ashore under the breadfruit trees. Being a chief, he was entertained by the chiefs in a manner befitting his station. He entered into all the sports of the Maui chiefs.

One day when the sea was smooth, Ku-a-nu'uanu went surfing with the other chiefs at Uo, the celebrated surfing place. There he showed his wonderful skill. He could gracefully ride the surfboard, standing or kneeling, and come to land without the spray even touching his body. Naturally his fame spread to all the islands.

After having spent two months on Maui, Ku-a-nu'uanu went to Oahu and landed at Waikiki, where the high chiefs lived. When it was known that the head servant of the king of Hawaii had come, the king of Oahu entertained him in royal fashion. He also ordered his people to bring clothing, mats, and food for the distinguished guest.

When Ku-a-nu'uanu had visited here for several weeks and had partaken of the kindness of the king, he decided to travel on to Kauai, where he landed at Kapa.

Near the sea he built himself a home and there men, women, and children flocked to see the stranger. In the midst of the crowd Ku-a-nu'uanu saw a very beautiful woman, who was called Laamaomao, and whom he at once longed to make his wife. Laamaomao consented and after twenty days they were married.

This marriage angered the parents of Laamaomao greatly, for, though they held a high social position through their relationship to the *kahuna*, nevertheless, they were very poor, and had hoped to marry their beautiful daughter to one of the wealthy princes of the island with whom they could live and spend their old age. Now, their daughter had married a tramp, a stranger with nothing, and they themselves were without food.

The princes of Kauai were also angry, as they had wished to win Laamaomao's hand, and so the stranger from Hawaii was hated by all.

Soon, however, Ku-a-nu'uamu had planted taro, potatoes, sugar cane, and bananas to provide food for his wife and her family. When they had lived thus for two months, a messenger from the king of Hawaii came to Ku-a-nu'uanu and said, "By the order of the king I come to take you home. The servants whom you left in your place are not skilled in providing for the king. Your lord says that you have traveled long enough."

Hearing these words, Ku-a-nu'uanu wept bitterly because his king was in trouble. At last he answered, "I will return with you. On this island I have married. I have planted food for my wife and her parents. It is not ripe yet. If I go my wife will be in great need. She will be forced to crawl to others' doors and beg for food. But my love for my king calls me. These bones are his. He has the power to take my head if he so chooses. I cannot disobey any of his commands."

That evening Ku-a-nu'uanu told Laamaomao that he must return to his king but she must stay on Kauai. He explained to her that he was not a common tramp as her parents believed, but a chief and the backbone of a king. To be known as the backbone of the king was the highest honor a chief could attain. He talked over the probable birth of a child to them, telling her to name a girl after her friends, but to name a boy Pakaa, which means the skin of his king cracked with drinking *awa*.

All these things made the beautiful Laamaomao weep bitterly, but she submitted to her cruel fate and the next day bade her husband aloha as he departed with the messenger.

After a time a boy was born to Laamaomao and she called him Pakaa, as she had been commanded by the father. The happy mother thought that now the anger of her parents would be appeased, but they refused to receive her and called the baby the child of a servant. They could not forget the plans they had made for their daughter to marry a chief of Kauai.

WILLIAM HYDE RICE

And so Laamaomao lived on alone where the *pali* rises from the sea at Kapaa, and there she brought up her boy.

When Mailou, Laamaomao's brother, who loved her dearly, saw how his sister was being treated, he stayed with her and helped her care for her boy. Mailou was very skillful in catching birds, as his name signifies, and in this way he made a living for them all.

At one time when they were in great trouble Laamaomao sent Mailou to her brothers and sisters begging for help. They provided for their outcast sister without letting their parents know.

As Pakaa grew older he began to wonder where his father was, and so one day, he asked his mother about him. The mother, not wishing to explain to the boy the father's going, told him that Mailou was his father. This the child would not believe, saying, "He cannot be my father. He is very small and I am very large."

After many such questions Laamaomao was forced to tell Pakaa the truth. She said to him, "Look where the sun rises. There your father lives. We feel the wind which is sent from there by the king, the keeper of all the winds."

So the boy believed his mother and resolved that when he became older he would seek his father.

Meanwhile he tried to increase his skill in all things which add to manhood. He became very skillful in farming, fishing, surfing, and hewing out canoes, but he decided to become a fisherman.

When the king's fishermen were driving the flying fish, Pakaa would follow the fishermen and they always gave him a few fish. He complained to his mother that he was given only a few fish while all the others received many. She told him that this was because the fishermen considered Mailou very lazy and did not want to help him.

Then Pakaa began to beg his mother to allow him to join the fishermen. She feared that he was too small and could not swim well enough. But the boy assured his mother that he could swim as well as any of the men. At last she promised to get her brother's canoe for the boy.

As Pakaa watched the fishermen he noticed how difficult it was to paddle the canoes out to the deep sea, so he tried to find a way to lessen the labor. Day and night be dreamed. At last a thought came to him. He found and cut two slender, straight sticks nine feet in length. Then he took a roll of *lauhala* and wove a small square mat. This finished, he tied its ends to the sticks, thus making a sail as he had dreamed of doing, so that his shoulders would not ache from paddling his canoe. Then the boy went home to await his uncle's return. Thus was the first sail made.

After Mailou had brought birds from the mountains the little family partook of the evening meal. Then Laamaomao told her brother that on the morning he must help lift Pakaa in his canoe into the sea. Mailou complained, saying that he was able to supply enough birds and that they did not need fish. Laamaomao, too, beginning again to fear for her child's safety, urged him to stay at home. But the boy, having the same determination which had led his mother to marry without her parent's consent, could not be dissuaded from his plan, and his elders reluctantly consented.

Early the next morning Mailou lifted the canoe into the water. Seeing the strange-looking *lauhala* mat, he asked the boy what it was. But Palas told him to wait and see. His uncle answered by saying that the fishermen would laugh at him if he went fishing with such a strange object. So the boy explained what it was, and setting up the mast, pushed out the boom The early morning breeze from the mountains filled the sail and carried the canoe along. Pakaa steered the canoe and it glided gracefully through the water as if it were a living thing.

Mailou was astonished. When he saw what the boy had done he called out to him that history would remember him as the first person to sail a canoe.

As Pakaa neared the fishermen, he concealed his sail. They were surprised to see the boy and wondered why his uncle had not come with him.

The drive of the flying fish began. Pakaa's canoe was in the middle of the fleet. He soon saw that the men on the outside, got the first fish caught in the nets, so he paddled to the outside. The older men called to him that his place was not there, but he went on lifting up the net and getting many fish. When they started home the boy had eighty fish in his canoe.

Pakaa urged the men to race to land, placing all the fish as the wager. After much wrangling, a large canoe paddled by eight men accepted the boy's challenge, first placing all their fish in his canoe, for he insisted that they might take advantage of his size and keep the fish, even though they lost the race.

The signal to start was given and in no time the eight paddlers left Pakaa far behind. When they saw the boy turning the bow of his boat

WILLIAM HYDE RICE

to the wind and arranging a mat they jeered at him and asked where his boasted strength was.

As soon as Pakaa had hoisted his sail, he turned his canoe toward land. The wind filled the sail and the canoe began to skim over the deep sea. When he neared the large boat, the men began to paddle with all their strength but the little canoe sailed quickly by them, and they heard the boy calling. "Use more strength so that sooner you may drink the water of Wailua. Pakaa, the firstborn, will eat the flying fish."

Pakax reached the dry sand long before the others and so the one hundred and sixty fish in the canoe were his. He shared them with the people who crowded around to see the strange sail, and who wondered at his cleverness. Then rolling up the sail, and putting the fish in a bag, Palas hurried home to tell his mother and uncle of his good fortune.

Laamaomao's happiness was very great and she said to her son, "I am rewarded for my care of you. You will bring life to my bones." Mailou was no less happy and it was a very cheerful family which that might enjoyed an evening meal of fish. Laamaomao did not forget her neighbors in her good fortune and they all were given some of the boy's first fish.

At this time Paica was king of Kauai. One day the desire to visit all the islands came to him, so he sent for his *kahuna* and soothsayers to learn from them the propitious time for starting on such a journey.

These wise men informed him that the time for such an undertaking was at hand, but they advised him first to travel around his own island, Kauai. This advice the king accepted.

Upon hearing of the king's intended journey, his retainers at Kapaa prepared to accompany him to Oahu, Maui, and Hawaii. Pakaa's interest in these preparations was intense, and he begged to be allowed to go with them. He won their consent and at last his mother's also, though she feared that the king might abuse her son.

When it became known that Paiea would visit his people, food and fish in abundance were prepared for the entertainment not only of the king but of his retainers and followers as well.

Six months were spent in traveling around Kauai, Pakaa followed the king and his retainers, doing errands cheerfully and humbly. When the divisions of food was made he was never given any, but so much was wasted by others that he always had enough to eat. He was determined to be so useful that the retainers would take him to the other islands.

As the time for leaving Kauai came near, Pakaa explained to his mother how eager he was to reach Hawaii where his father lived. And the mother wisely advised her son to go in meekness and not in pride, willing to serve others. Thus would he come to the valley of Waipio, on Hawaii, where his father dwelt with the king.

There, she said, "You will see two aged, white-haired men, the king wearing a feather cloak and lei, and your father, holding a kahili. Without fear, sit on your father's lap, tell him that you are Pakaa, and then he will receive you and grant you all the blessings of life, property, and honor. At last, my child, you will come into your own as the son of the chief of Hawaii and the backbone of the king."

Having spoken these words Laamaomao gave Pakaa a very finely polished calabash in a *koko*, or net which she said contained the bones of his grandmother, Loa, and also the winds which blow from Hawaii and the winds which blow from Kaula, Bird Island. Pakaa took the calabash, and in surprise heard his mother say, "In her life your grandmother controlled the winds. Before her death she put all the winds into this calabash and gave it to me. She told me that after her death her bones were to be concealed in the calabash with the winds. This I was to keep carefully until my son should need it. Now I place it in your keeping. You will find it very useful on your journey. If becalmed, you can summon any wind you wish. If ridiculed, open the calabash and call for a fair wind which will carry you safely to land. This power to control the winds will win you much fame with kings."

Then Laamaomao taught Pakaa the names of all the winds and the prayers and *mele* used with each. Thus was her only son prepared to go in search of the father he had never seen.

In the meantime Paica had collected a great crowd of high and low chiefs, retainers, and followers. So many canoes were needed to transport this crowd that when they put to sea the water between Kauai and Oahu became calm. The canoes looked like a great mass of clouds.

This fleet of canoes landed at Waikiki where the king was entertained with great pomp. After a few days Paiea went on to Molokai and Maui and came finally to Hawaii where a landing was made at Kohala. Here the people became alarmed upon seeing so many canoes and, believing it to be a battle fleet, prepared to attack the enemy.

However, as soon as they recognized Paiea they sent word to their king, who ordered messengers to conduct him to Waipio. There he was given a great welcome. The people gladly brought presents of food so that the guests from Kauai had more than they could eat. That day the smoke from the many *imu* where pigs, chickens, taro, and bananas were cooking, obscured the sun.

This hospitality did not last. The streams which had poured in food began to grow dry. Want came and Paiea's followers had to hunt food for themselves. So it always was. The first days of the stranger's visit were over supplied, the last days were neglected.

As the days went by and the shortage of food came, Pakaa, everybody's slave, was often hungry. Looking at the king and his chief advisor the boy would greatly amuse the crowd by saying, "If I can reach those two old men yonder I can have all I want." For these words he was ridiculed. How could he ever hope to reach men so well guarded? Did he not know that to go into the king's presence meant death?

But Pakaa waited for his opportunity. One day he put on a fresh *malo* and tapa and watched for a moment when the soldiers were not looking. In an unguarded second he passed them and ran rapidly to his father and jumped onto his lap.

Among the old Hawaiians it was the law of the land that only his own child could sit on his father's lap. So Ku-a-nu'nanu asked the name of this boy who had dared to break the *kapu*. When he heard the name, Pakaa, he knew that this was his son, born to the beloved wife he had left on Kauai and named by her as he had ordered. He pressed the boy to his heart and wept bitterly for the absent mother.

Then he told the king of his marriage on Kauai. The king was delighted with Pakaa and said, "You must teach your son all you know so that if you sleep the long sleep before I do he can care for me." Messengers were sent to order the people to bring gifts for Pakaa, the king's new steward. They came with great rejoicing, carrying many presents of food and clothing.

When Paiea and his followers saw into what a position Pakaa had fallen, they were afraid, for they recalled their unkind treatment of the boy. But Pakaa was forgiving and gladly divided all his gifts among the king and his retainers, according to the social standing of each person.

So the son of Laamaomao had come into his own. As he grew in stature he became very handsome. In cultivation of the land, in navigation, in fishing, in astrology, Pakaa excelled all others. This skill brought him great favor with the king who gave him lands. Many of Paiea's retainers preferred to stay with him when their king returned to Kauai, and so he became next to the highest chief on Hawaii.

In his good fortune Pakaa did not forget his mother and when Paiea went home he sent canoes loaded with gifts to her. Many times afterwards he sent canoe loads of presents to her, so that her days of want were ended. In adversity Laamaomao had had no friends. In prosperity many claimed relationship with her and attached themselves to her household.

When Pakaa had reached his twenty-fifth year his father fell ill. The *kahuna* who were summoned said that nothing could be done for him. Knowing that death was near, the faithful old chief called his son to his side and said, "My days on earth are growing few. I leave my king in your care. Listen to his commands at all times. Care for the food which is not eaten. Dry it and place it in calabashes. Care for the fish and the growing *awa*. Care for the king's subjects, high and low."

After death had claimed Ku-a-nu'uanu there was great mourning in the land. The king and all his subjects wept bitterly for him, the most beloved of all on Hawaii. When the days of mourning were over Pakaa took his father's place. He was made head chamberlain, diviner, treasurer and navigator. He became the *iwi-kua-moo*, the backbone of the king.

At this time Kahikuokamoku, the prime minister, divided the government of the island into five sections, each section being placed under a chief. Under this system and Pakaa's guidance, Hawaii was at peace. The high and low loved Pakaa dearly, as he was very just in all his dealings. The king loved him because he had even more ability than his father.

However, as always happens, Pakaa had enemies who tried to undermine him with the king. These were two men, Hookele-i-hilo, Navigator-to-Hilo, and Hookele-i-puna, Navigator-to-Puna, skillful navigators who could sail the seas and who could foretell weather conditions. In fact they knew almost as much about navigation as Pakaa did, but they lacked the calabash of winds. They wished for themselves the power and honor that belonged to the youthful Pakaa. So at every opportunity they complained and lied to the king about Pakaa and boasted of their own ability.

Little by little the king was deceived by these lies and began to turn against his faithful servant, who never dreamed what was going on. At last the time came when the king took away all Pakaa's canoes and all his land except two small lots, giving these possessions into the keeping of the boy's enemies. Pakaa was now only treasurer of the king and caretaker of his houses.

Poor Pakaa was sore at heart, for he knew that he was unjustly

WILLIAM HYDE RICE

treated. Soon the chiefs followed the king's example and gave him no honor and tried to find fault with him. Then Pakaa decided to go away. He placed some of the king's most beautiful *malo* in the calabash with the winds and set forth in his canoe.

When his enemies saw him leaving they tried to capsize his canoe, but he escaped probable death by lashing mats to the canoe. Fortunately a fair wind followed him and he reached Hilo safely where his cousin, Lapakahoe, the Flash-of-the-Paddle, was living, taking charge of Pakaa's lands there. Pakaa explained to Lapakahoe that he had fallen into disfavor and was going away from Hawaii and the enemies he had unwittingly made. So, alone, the discouraged Pakaa paddled his canoe and came in due time to Molokai, where a strange fate lay in wait for him.

On Molokai lived a very beautiful woman, Hikauhi, the daughter of Hoolehua and Ilali. Now it happened that the girl's father had promised her hand to Palaau, the chief of that part of the island. But as soon as she had seen Pakaa, she forgot all about her former lover and demanded that the stranger begiven to her. Palaau very generously consented, and so they all lived in peace. Pakaa cultivated the lands well, fished skillfully, and brought great prosperity to his wife and her family.

When a son was born to Hikanhi, Pakaa named him Ku-a-pakaa, Standing-in-the-Place-of-Pakaa, for his father and his grandfather. This child was brought up very carefully. His father taught him all the *mele* be had made for the king of Hawaii, for he believed that in time the king would miss him and would send for him, and he wanted the boy to be prepared. He also taught the boy the names of all the winds of the islands as his mother, Laamaomao, had taught him long before.

In the meantime things were not going very smoothly with the king of Hawaii. At first his new servants had taken very good care of him but soon they became careless. After Pakaa had been gone several months, the king realized that these men were working only for themselves and were neglecting him sorely. He was patient as long as he could be, but at last he decided to go in search of his faithful Pakaa. Summoning his soothsayers, his *kahuna*, and his diviners he asked them where to find Pakaa. They communed with the spirits of their ancestors and learned that Pakaa was still living, but his dwelling place was not known to them. They urged the king to delay his departure until a large fleet of canoes had been hewn out.

So the king ordered all his people to join the canoe cutters and to hurry to the mountains. All those who were not able to go must prepare the food supply. The king hoped that these preparations could be easily and quickly made. He was doomed to disappointment.

As soon as the first tree had been cut, two birds flew upon the branches, which was a sign that the tree was hollow. A second tree was cut, and again it was seen to be hollow. The cutters went from tree to tree, always with the same result.

Then the king sent for the skilled sling throwers and the net catchers and the gum catchers but they were all unable to catch the two birds who were, in fact, ancestors of Pakaa, and who were trying to prove the king's aloha for the boy.

At last from Kauai came Pikoi-a-kaalala, the Ambitious-One, the most skilled of all in shooting the bow and arrow. He could shoot off the head of a flower. He never missed a bird on the fly.

The king greeted Pikoi warmly and made known to him the trouble he was having with the birds. Taking his bow and arrow, the skillful hunter hurried to the forest where the trees were being cut down and shot both birds. In vain he looked for the bodies of the troublesome birds. However, with the shooting of them, all difficulty was removed and two beautiful canoes were soon prepared for the king, and others were made ready for his retainers.

In the meantime, on Molokai, Pakaa had heard that the king was about to set forth to find him. This news pleased Pakaa very much and that night he dreamed that the spirit of the king came to him and told him that he was searching for him. In his dream Pakaa told the king that he would find him at Kaula. When he awoke and recalled his dream Pakaa was very sorry that he had directed the king wrongly. He decided that if his former lord passed Molokai, he would urge him to land there, for he knew that his son would be a great help to him. He also plotted in his heart revenge on his two enemies.

Now it happened that Pakaa's house was too small to entertain the king and his retainers, and so Pakaa took his son with him into the mountains where they cut down trees to build larger houses. In a short time they had finished six houses of pili grass, one for each division of the island of Hawaii.

As soon as the houses were finished Pakaa and his son planted six ridges of sweet potatoes and six of sugar cane so that the king would have enough to eat. The king's delay because of the birds gave Pakaa ample time to finish his plans for the king's entertainment.

On the night before the king was to leave Hawaii he dreamed that

WILLIAM HYDE RICE

Pakaa's spirit came to him and said that he would find him on Kaula. In the morning all the *kahuna*, and paddlers, and steerers were summoned and told the dream. They declared that Pakaa was not on Kaula. The king dreamed again that Pakaa was on Kaula. When his kahuna still insisted that the dream was not true, the king decided to land on each island so that he could not miss his beloved servant.

At last the canoes set out, the single canoes leading, the double canoes with supplies following. Next were the canoes with the head soldiers, the women, the common soldiers. Then came the six chiefs, followed last of all by the king and his prime minister. A stately fleet whose going showed how well the king loved Pakaa.

The first landing was made at Lahaina. There it was learned that Pakaa did not live on Maui, so the fleet went on. When Pakaa saw the canoes leaving Mani he called his son to go fishing with him. They got into their canoe, Pakaa sitting in the bow with his head so bowed that the king could not recognize him, the boy paddling. As they neared the fishing grounds they caught the first glimpse of the king's fleet. As the canoes came nearer Pakaa recognized those belonging to the six chiefs who were not real chiefs and whom he ridiculed by calling out, "You are an under-chief. You hid behind the sugar cane and ate sugar cane. And you also are only an eel catcher." So he ridiculed all the chiefs in order to arouse their anger.

Ku-a-pakaa was anxious to know when the king would pass by, and his father told him that when the sun rose the king would come in a double canoe. On the *pola* of the canoe would be seen a large house for the king's god, Kaili, the Snatcher, a small one for himself, and a still smaller one for the women.

At last the king's canoe appeared and Pakaa called out, "As you pass by hold up your paddle, Lapakahoe."

These words were told to the king by his messenger and the pilots received orders to approach Pakaa's canoe. As they neared Pakaa, he told his son to ask them to come ashore as a storm was coming. He also bade the boy ask them whom they were seeking. To this question someone answered, "We seek Pakaa, a servant of the king."

This answer surprised Ku-a-pakaa, who said to his father, "They say that you are a servant. You told me you were a chief."

Pakaa told his son to ask the question again, and this time he received this answer from the king, "He is not a real servant. He is a kahili bearer and my backbone."

This answer made Ku-a-paaka very happy and he sang a *mele* in which he said that these canoes must be made from the great Hawaii of Kane, where the sun rises from the point of Haehae bringing aloha to the king, a friend in days of want when there is no food on the land.

The prime minister answered the boy's *mele* in these words, "Do you not see, O boy, that these are the canoes of Ku and Lono, of Kane and Kanaloa, and all the multitude of gods? These canoes came from Hilo, the land of heavy rain, which makes the leaves fall from the trees. The land where leis are made from the *hala* blossoms of Hapae."

Now Ku-a-pakaa began to sing *mele* urging the canoes to come ashore as the clouds brought by the winds from Ha-o and Ha-ea were gathering on Kawainui, above Wailau, which foretold a storm.

But the king's pilot answered, "Why should we listen to this boy? If we go ashore the canoes will be cracked and we will take the boy's bones to stop the leaks."

Pakaa told his son to reply in this manner, "No one fills the cracks of canoes with the bones of a boy. Everyone takes a stone adz and cuts down a tree. When the tree is felled he cuts off the branches and then hews out the canoe. The bones of a dog or a pig are used to give polish to the canoe."

The king's companions were surprised to hear the boy answer so wisely. Thinking that he probably knew the weather signs of his own island, the prime minister asked him to tell them.

Ku-a-pakaa replied, "A storm will come. The wind will turn your canoes around and bring you back. So far, the wind from Hawaii has helped you. Soon an adverse wind will roughen the sea."

Then Ku-a-pakaa recited the names of all the winds of Hawaii, and also all the winds of Oahu and Kanai. When asked how he happened to know all the winds he answered that all the boys knew them.

To this one of the paddlers cried out, "That is not true. Only two people know all the winds, my cousin, Pakaa, and I. Do you know where Pakaa is? Is he on this island?"

But the boy would not tell the hiding place of his father, saying that he had heard that it was on Kaula.

When the prime minister asked who was in the bow of his canoe the boy replied, "That is my father who is deaf and does not hear your words."

All this delay was very annoying to the paddlers who were anxious to be off, even though their king urged them to go ashore. They vowed that if they ever reached Oahu safely, they would return and put the impudent boy to death.

The king was very much interested in the boy and asked his name. "Come ashore and you shall hear my name," was the only answer he received.

In spite of all his efforts the boy was unable to persuade the paddlers to land. So he tried something more powerful than words. Opening his calabash of winds he called, "Blow winds from Kauai against them. Blow winds of Oahu and Hawaii from the side. Blow winds of Maui and Molokai behind them."

At once the clouds arose, the heavens became dark, the thunder roared, the lightning flashed, and the sea became very rough.

When the king saw these signs of bad weather he was very angry with his paddlers who had told him that clear weather would prevail. He called out, "The wind is coming, the stones are rolling, a great storm is at hand. I urged you to listen to the boy, but you only ridiculed him. Now the deep sea will engulf us and we shall be lost. Would that we had gone ashore."

No sooner had he spoken than the storm struck the first canoes, capsizing some of them and the strong current carried many of the sailors away. Soon the sea filled all the canoes. As the king's canoes went to the help of the smaller ones death came very near to the great king of Hawaii. The sea washed away the food and fish and clothing. The men and their king clung to the canoes though they were chilled to the bone by the cold rain. Then the king in anger called for Pakaa, his beloved servant, the only person who could take him safely on a journey.

As soon as Pakaa saw the sad plight of the king he ordered his son to close the calabash of winds. At once the sea became calm. The sun shone brightly. The sailors swam back to their canoes and began to bail out the water.

The king looked about and seeing that Molokai was the only land near them, he ordered the canoes to return to the place where the boy was fishing.

As the canoes approached, Pakaa told his son to say that the entrance to their harbor was very crooked. If they would enter it safely they must follow him.

Reaching the boy the king called out, "It came to pass as you said. The storm rose and our canoes were badly damaged. Now we have come back to you for help."

Remembering his father's warning Ku-a-pakaa replied, "If you had come into the harbor when I warned you there would have been no danger. Now the tide is high and we must go carefully or your canoes will be cast on the rocks and you will have none with which to find Pakaa or to return to Hawaii."

So they followed the boy, and the first canoes safely reached the sandy beach.

No sooner had Pakaa's canoe touched land than he jumped ashore and ran as quickly as possible to the house where he had stored the food, for he hoped to hide himself there. It happened that Lapakahoe saw him running and noticed how much he resembled Pakaa.

By evening of this day all the canoes had returned and were safely landed. The king sat on the *pola*, wet and unhappy, for all his clothing had been lost.

Seeing the king's sad state Ku-a-pakaa hurried to his father and told him. Pakaa sent the king's own clothing, which he had brought with him from Hawaii, to the unhappy king who was surprised to see clothing which so much resembled his own. He gave the boy his wet malo which he carried to his father. Pakaa hung it over the door, so that no one would dare to enter the room made *kapu* by the king's clothing.

Pakaa also sent to his king the tapas he had brought from Hawaii, telling his son to say that his mother had made them and scented them with sweet smelling herbs.

As with the *malo* the king thought that the tapa looked familiar and remarked, "Only on Hawaii is this tapa made. Pakaa always took care of my tapas. Can he be on this island?"

But the boy replied that his mother had made them in an inaccessible valley for him, her only son and a high chief.

Ku-a-pakaa directed each of the six chiefs to the houses which had been prepared by his father and where nothing was lacking for his comfort.

The king was waited upon by the boy whose adroitness very much pleased him. As night fell the boy heard him say, "My aloha for Pakaa is great. At this time of evening he was wont to prepare the sweet *awa* that brought happy dreams. Together we drank and then lay down to sleep."

These words Ku-a-pakaa told to his father, who at once sent his to the king with the ata strainer, the prepared area, and a large piece of *awa* root. When the king ordered him to chew the *awa* the boy was to pretend to do so, but instead he was to give him the prepared *awa*. This

WILLIAM HYDE RICE

would be done so quickly that the king would be greatly pleased. Then he was to run to the sea and bring live fish for the king.

Ku-a-pakaa did all these things as he was told and the king's admiration was great, for the boy had done his work like a man. Happier than he had been for sometime, the king drank the *awa* and lay down to happy dreams. All his followers, wearied by events of the day, followed his example and soon sleep claimed them all.

As they slept, Ku-a-pakaa released some of the winds and a great storm arose which would delay their going.

Then Pakaa and his son counseled together how they could destroy the king's two navigators who had so unjustly taken Pakaa's place.

After much thought Pakaa explained his plan to his son thus, "Take this hollow log to your grandfather's house. When the food which we have supplied for each chief is gone we shall give each one a ridge planted with potatoes. Ask them not to throw away any of the small potatoes. These must be cooked and given to your grandfather, who will store them carefully away in the hollow log. He will also store away dried fish and will fill the gourds with water. When the day for leaving comes the king will urge you to accompany him. Consent if he allows you to take your bundle with you. Besides the log you must take a large stone fastened to a coil of rope. After you have passed through the channel between Oahu and Kauai and have neared Waimea, release some stormy winds from the calabash. Then cast the stone into the sea and anchor the canoes. When the cold winds have chilled the men, give all but my two enemies a palm leaf to shield themselves from the rain. Also give them dried fish, potatoes, and water. Keep doing this until the two navigators are chilled almost to death. Then cover the calabash of winds and take the king back to Hawaii."

The boy listened carefully to his father's words and prepared to do as he was told.

When the stormy month of February had passed one of the chiefs reported to the king that their food was all gone. The king then summoned Ku-a-pakaa and asked for food. The boy told the king that he had six hills of potatoes and six hills of sugar cane on the uplands ready for him.

"How can six hills of potatoes and six hills of sugar cane supply my many people?" asked the king.

The boy answered that when the potatoes and cane saw the number of people, they would bear abundantly, and so all the people must go up into the highlands. He told this tale so that the lazy ones would work.

The king sent only half the men to do the work. They were surprised when they saw the fields of potatoes and sugar cane stretching away farther than the eye could reach. Messengers were sent for the rest of the men and they were all soon busy digging. Ku-a-pakaa told them to take all, big and small, for he wanted the small ones dried. "You will have eaten all my growing food during the stormy months and I must have dried food until I can plant some more," he explained, wishing to keep his father's plan secret.

At last when all preparations were made the calabash was closed and the sea became calm. Ku-a-pakaa ordered the chiefs to lash the canoes together and to float them in the bay, ready to sail them when the morning star appeared. They lay down to sleep until the king's crier should awaken them.

Very early Ku-a-pakaa called them saying, "Awake! Awake! It is halfway between night and day. Your weariness is gone. The morning star is rising."

When they realized that it was only the boy calling them, they were very angry and refused to get up. But he kept calling them until at last be aroused them, and the six chiefs left without their king. They had had so little sleep that when they lay off Leahi, Diamond Head, they fell asleep. Then the winds were sent which turned their canoes around and drove them back to the coast of Hawaii. There they met their families and there was great rejoicing for they had been given up as lost.

Meantime on Molokai the king and his followers slept until day dawned. Then the king sent for Ku-a-pakaa and asked him to go with them. At first the boy refused, saying that he must stay with his old people. At last he consented to go if he could take his bundles with him. The king sent two messengers for these bundles. The messengers were greatly surprised when they saw a heavy stone and the hollow log as long as the canoe.

"The king would never have consented to take your bundles if he had seen their size. You are indeed a strange boy to call a stone and a log bundles. We have been working for the king from childhood up and we have never seen bundles like these," cried one messenger.

To this complaint Ku-a-pakaa answered, "Did you not bring women with you? Were they not like stones which never work?"

And so the messengers carried the strange bundles to the paddlers, who were very angry and said that the king would refuse to take them. But the king did not interfere, and at last the bundles were loaded on the canoe.

Then Ku-a-pakaa hurried to the hiding place of his father and told him that everything was ready. Pakaa urged his son to remember all that he had made known to him.

"I am only a boy. If I am killed it is well. If I kill your enemies then you will be avenged," was the son's reply to his father.

So he returned to the king and a fair wind drove the canoes gently along. The skill of the paddlers pleased the boy greatly and he asked to hold one of the paddles but was refused.

After they had passed Oahu and lay off Waimea on Kauai, Ku-a-pakaa opened his calabash of winds and released some stormy winds which quickly blew the canoes out to sea. As before, the sea grew angry, and great waves dashed against the canoes, driving them out to the deep water. But the king was not afraid. Peace filled his mind because Ku-a-pakaa was with him. When the king asked what to do, the boy replied, "Anchor the canoe with my big stone which will keep us in one place, so that we shall not be blown out of sight of land. When the storm is over we can reach land."

Then the boy carried out all the plans his father had so carefully made known to him.

He gave food and water to the men. He gave them the palm leaves to protect themselves against the wind. The two enemies of his father were given nothing. The enemies realized that death would probably overtake them, but they patiently suffered and asked for nothing. As Ku-a-pakaa saw them growing colder and colder, he knew that his father would soon be avenged.

At last Hookele-i-hilo fell into the sea. The people cried, "Alas!" but they were too busy saving themselves to grieve. Soon Hookele-i-puna followed his friend and again the people exclaimed, "Alas!" So these two false friends of the king died the death they had plotted for Pakaa.

When Ku-a-pakaa knew that his father's enemies were dead he covered his calabash and at once the sea became calm. The king asked him to take the place of the dead navigators, and so the boy was in command.

The sun shone brightly and, warming up the king and his followers, son put them all to sleep. Then Ku-a-pakaa turned the canoe toward Molokai and released from the calabash a fair wind which carried them swiftly along.

At dawn the king was surprised to find the canoe lying off Hawaii. Great excitement prevailed in the canoe and on land, for often it had seemed that there would be no returning.

The men in the canoe were anxious to land at once. Ku-a-pakaa knew that in the glad homecoming he would be forgotten and so, indeed, it came to pass. Each man was welcomed by his own. The great crowd was filled with joy to see the king again. As soon as the wailing and the reciting of *mele* was ended all hurried to their homes. No one thought of the boy who was left alone in the canoe. As he saw the smoke rising from the *imu* he realized how hungry he was, and hoped that someone would remember him. But the king thought the people were caring for him and the people thought that he was surely with the king.

Thus it happened that Ku-a-pakaa found himself at evening alone and forgotten. He prepared to spend the night in the canoe and to eat what he could find in the hollow log. Great loneliness filled his heart and he longed for his home.

For several days the boy saw no one. Then he heard the head fisherman ordering all the men to prepare the canoes for a flying fish drive. He asked to be allowed to accompany them, promising to bail out the water and not to claim any share in the fish caught. So it came about that Ku-a-pakaa, plotting much in his heart, was taken into one of the canoes.

The fish drive was very successful. Each man was given forty fish and started for his own landing. Ku-a-pakaa, paddling with two companions, saw a larger canoe with six paddlers. He at once challenged this canoe to a race, the fish being placed as the wager. His friends were not eager to paddle against so many, so he told them to join the others and he would paddle alone. He took the precaution his father had taken so many years before of insisting that all the fish be placed in his canoe.

Then the race began. At first the eight paddlers quickly outdistanced the one. But Ku-a-pakaa prayed to his grandmother, "Give me a large surf so that I can reach the shore safely. Then we shall eat flying fish together."

Looking back he saw a huge wave which carried him swiftly to shore and landed him safely on the sand. Then he carried all the fish to the king's canoe where he concealed them.

The paddlers in the larger canoe feared to ride such a big surf. They felt sure that the boy would wreck his canoe. So they waited until the quiet water followed the big wave and then they paddled ashore. When they saw that all the fish were gone they were very angry and challenged the boy to another race.

Ku-a-pakaa consented to a second race, but said that he had nothing to wager. They replied that they would wager their bones. The boy said, "I do not want to wager my bones. I am a wanderer here. I have no friends. If you lose the race and are killed your families and friends will wail for you. I'll wager those two double canoes yonder."

"But those canoes belong to the king. How can you wager them?" they asked.

The boy replied, "The king was a passenger with me. I have cared for the canoes for many days." Still they insisted that only bodies should be wagered and at last Ku-a-palaa consented, saying that no blame could be placed on him for laying this wager.

They set the day of Kau, Midsummer Day, for the race. Each contestant was to have a canoe six fathoms long. The loser was to pay the penalty by death in an ima. Ku-a-pakaa, knowing that these eight fishermen had received positions at the hands of his father's enemies, saw his father's complete revenge growing nearer.

The story of the coming race spread all over the island. Eight fishermen had been beaten by a small unknown boy! They would again try their luck on the day of Kau! Such was the news which reached the king's ears and great was his astonishment, for strange as it may seem, he never once remembered the wonderful boy who had saved his life.

People gathered from all over Hawaii to see the race. Men, women, and children hurried to the place of interest bringing with them pigs, dogs, feather cloaks, tapas, and other things. A few wanted to wager on the boy; many risked everything on the eight fishermen.

As the sun rose on the day of Kau, it saw the king's fishermen lifting their canoe into the water, preparing the *imu* and collecting the wood to cook their victim. When everything was prepared they called Ku-a-pakaa to begin the race.

But the boy replied, "First we must have ready two surfboards. The ones who reach the shore first must come in on the surfboard four times."

The fishermen were so eager to be off that they consented. In their excitement the length of the course was not determined upon. So they paddled out until they could just see the tops of the houses. Ku-a-pakaa had asked to stop before this, but they would not listen to him.

As they turned their canoes around the boy said to them, "If you had chosen a shorter course you might have beaten me. Now I shall win. Already I feel pity for your families."

The command to start was given. In their excitement the king's fishermen did not paddle together as skilled paddlers. Seeing their confusion, Ku-a-pakaa knew that he would win. He followed in the swell of their canoe, having only to steer his canoe. When the fishermen saw him close behind them they paddled with might and main.

"Paddle! Paddle for your lives!" called out Ku-a-pakaa.

As the canoes neared the shore the crowd saw the king's fishermen ahead and a shout of joy went up from their friends. But the fishermen were very weary. Some had dropped their paddles; some had no strength left to lift the paddles which hung from their hands. Then the boy shot ahead and the cry, "The boy is ahead! He is winning!" aroused anger in the hearts of those who were supporting the king's fishermen.

After Ku-a-pakaa had touched land, he ran for a surfboard and rode the breakers four times as had been arranged.

When the eight fishermen had brought their canoe ashore, they threw themselves on the sand and bitterly regretted having wagered their bones. They saw the *imu* ready to receive them and knew that death would soon be their fate. A great aloha for their wives, and children, and friends filled their hearts. They wept bitterly as they saw the unknown boy collecting the rich rewards of his victory.

A messenger had hurried to the king with the news of the boy's victory. Then the king remembered the boy who had saved his life and had brought him safely back to Hawaii, and so he sent his servant to conduct the boy to him.

Ku-a-pakaa gladly hurried into the king's presence. At once the king recognized the boy who had saved him from a bitter death at sea and called him to come before him. The boy, remembering the *kapu*, hesitated, but the king removed the *kapu* and Ku-a-pakaa crawled before him. The king embraced him and wept over him, regretting that he had forgotten him in his happy return home.

Then the head steward was called to prepare a meal of the best food from the king's own table. As Ku-a-pakaa ate he told the king how he had lived in the canoe, eating the food left from the voyage.

"*Auwe, auwe!*" cried the king. "Unhappy man that I am to have thus rewarded one who saved my bones and brought me home from a strange land. You foretold that you would be left where the canoes were drawn up and so it has come about. It is my fault and not the fault of my men. Is it you who raced with my eight fishermen? Tell me the wager."

Ku-a-pakaa told him that in the first race the wager had been their fish, in the second it had been their bones. He continued, "When I left the shore the *imu* was being prepared. The men are to be thrown in when it is red hot."

The king wept bitterly for his men. The boy told him that this wager was of their own choosing. He had wanted to wager canoes.

The king cried, "O boy, if you have aloha for me, spare the lives of my eight fishermen who supply me with fish. They are very skillful and never go out without bringing in fish."

To this prayer the boy answered, "I do love you, but I must not spare the lives of these men. If you wish to see Pakaa again you cannot spare the lives of these men."

The king replied, "Bring Pakaa to me. When I see him I shall consent to the death of my fishermen."

"Do you recall the first time we met at sea?" asked the boy. "You saw an old man sitting in the bow of my canoe. That was Pakaa. He did not wish to return to Hawaii until his enemies were killed. I am Pakaa's son. My name is Ku-a-pakaa—so named from the cracks in your skin. The tapas which I gave you when you were wet from the sea were those that my father had carried with him from Hawaii."

The king was filled with delight at these words, for he knew that he would see his beloved Pakaa again. He ordered his eight fishermen thrown into the *imu*. He started the boy off for Molokai at once to bring Pakaa to him.

When Ku-a-pakaa had left Molokai with the king, his mother had bitterly reproached his father for allowing their only child to go away from them. She knew that death at sea would overtake her only son. Pakaa told her not to grieve for the boy would return. He urged her to look towards Maui and she would soon see the mast sail of a canoe. The canoe would belong to the boy who had sent death to the two navigators and the eight fishermen. Then they would know that all those who had estranged him from the king were dead.

All these assurances of her son's safety failed to lessen the mother's anxiety. Nevertheless, she spent her days looking for the mast sail of a canoe. At last she saw it. Father and mother were overcome with joy. As their son stepped ashore his mother pressed him to her heart.

Pakaa heard the story of the boy's adventures from the day he had left Molokai until his return. When he heard the king's command that he return to Hawaii he asked, "What gifts did the king give you?"

"He gave me nothing," replied Ku-a-pakaa. "He will give you bountiful gifts when you return."

"Without promised gifts there is no use in my returning," answered Pakaa. "Better that I stay on Molokai, where I have something to call my own."

In vain Ku-a-pakaa urged his father to return with him to care for the king who had lost all his servants. Pakaa said that when the king had restored his position and lands, then only would he return.

Ku-a-pakaa stayed with his parents for three days, resting and preparing to go back to the king. When he had not returned by the evening of the second day, the king sent his prime minister with many canoes to conduct Pakaa and his son back to Hawaii.

When the sun had reached its zenith on the third day, Pakaa saw the canoes nearing the land and he knew that the king had sent for his son.

As Lapakahoe, now the prime minister, saw his cousin, Pakaa, he threw his arms about him and they wailed together. After this greeting the prime minister asked his old friend why he had not made himself known to the king before. Pakaa replied that he had wanted to test the king's aloha for him and to get his revenge on those who had wronged him.

Then he called his wife, the daughter of a chief of Molokai, whom he had married when he had come as a stranger to the island, and introduced her to the king's men.

Pakaa promised to return to Hawaii if the king would restore his lands and position. The prime minister promised all in the name of the king, and with his canoes loaded with gifts set out for home.

When the king saw his men returning without Pakaa he was very sad. But when he had heard Pakaa's promise he ordered his men to prepare a fleet of two hundred canoes to go for his beloved servant. He kept Ku-a-pakaa with him.

As this great fleet neared Molokai, the people there thought that it must be a fleet fishing for flying fish. But they soon realized that it had come for Pakas, who returned to Hawaii like a king with friends and retainers. His king wept over him and gave him position and lands befitting so faithful a servant. So Pakaa lived in peace and honor for many years.

WILLIAM HYDE RICE

HOLUA-MANU

A Legend of Kauai

MANU, BIRD, LIVED WITH HIS parents in the mountains above Waimea valley. His greatest delight was to slide down the steep *pali* sides on his sled.

This sport caused his parents a great deal of worry, for they feared that he would meet with some accident. So they placed two immense rocks on the path he used most. But Manu could not be stopped by this. He jumped over the rocks, and struck the path below. However, he did not enjoy the jar, so he climbed back, and rolled one of the rocks down to the river, where it stands today, as large as a house.

Manu's parents prevented his crossing the river by sending a freshet to stop him. The freshet would start at the same moment that Manu stared to slide and it would always reach the river first.

At last discouraged, Manu took his sled, and went to the highest *pali* of the Waimea valley, where he enjoyed his sport, without interruption. This spot is still called Ka-holua-manu, or the Slide-of-Manu.

The Girl and the Mo-o

A Legend of Kauai

LIVING AT HOLUA-MANU IN THE mountains above Makaweli, was a family in which there was one child, a girl, who caused her parents much annoyance by her continuous crying. In a cave beneath a waterfall nearby lived a mo-o, which looked like a huge lizard or crocodile. One day when the child was crying as usual, her father in anger pushed her out of the house, saying thoughtlessly, "Go to the *mo-o* and live with him."

The child hurried to the cave and was welcomed by the *mo-o* who gladly cared for her and carefully brought her up. On warm, sunny days the girl and the monster would come out above the waterfall and sun themselves. If anyone approached, the mo-o would jump over the fall into the cave, and the girl would spring through a hole which led into it.

As the years went by the girl's parents grew more and more anxious to recover their child. Asking advice of the *kahuna*, they were told to cover the hole above the waterfall with a net, to trap her. One day they did as they were told. Soon the *mo-o* and the girl came out. The parents approached and the mo-o safely jumped over the waterfall, but the girl was caught in the net. Realizing that there was no escape for her, she cried, "In my youth you drove me from you. The *mo-o* cared for me. Now, why do you want me again?"

She was like a wild animal, struggling to be free. Not daring to keep her so near the cave the parents moved to Waimea, where gradually they tamed the girl, until she grew accustomed to her old life. She had become very beautiful and later she was married to the prince of Waimea.

Namaka O-Ka-Opae

A Legend of Kauai

There lived at Holua-manu a woman whose husband had been enticed away by another. Seeking advice, the unhappy wife went to her grandmother, who was a *kahuna*, living at the mouth of a little valley near Holua-manu. The grandmother told her to bring two ti leaves and she would show her how to destroy her rival.

When the girl returned her grandmother noticed that she had two stalks of ti instead of two leaves, so she tore off the leaves she wanted and threw the stalks away. One fell to the right of a little waterfall nearby and one to the left where they are growing to this day.

Then the old woman gave these instructions to the girl, "Take these leaves. Make them clean, and glossy and smooth. Place them on the crest of the waterfall. Go below and sit perfectly still on the rocks. Wait there until you rival comes. When she comes she will pick up a stone to throw at you. Not seeing the glossy ti leaves, she will slip on them and fall at your feet."

The miserable wife quickly followed out her grandmother's instructions and in a short time her rival was lying at her feet. Snatching a large stone she threw it on to the woman's stomach and killed her. Today in the clear water of the stream is seen a rock in the shape of a woman on whose stomach still lies the rock thrown by the angry wife.

After having killed her rival, the wife tore out the eyes from the dead body and, wrapping them in ti leaves, she threw them into the water. Then she followed the stream until she came to a second small waterfall under which she saw her husband sitting. She dropped a rock on his head which crushed in his skull and left his mouth wide open. By this time her rival's eyes had floated down stream. She placed the eyes in her husband's mouth, saying, "Here is your meat."

He was also turned to stone, and this rock, lying in the stream, can still be seen by passersby. From the ledge above, it looks like the crushed in skull of a man, with open mouth, and bulging eyes that glitter still as if alive. By the Hawaiians, this rock is still called Namaka-o-ka-opae, the Eyes-of-the-Shrimp.

KANA

A Legend of Hawaii

KANA WAS THE GRANDSON OF Uli, the supernatural woman who was married to the god Ku. Uli was born in Hilo. One of her brothers, Manu-a, lived in the underworld. Another brother, Wakea, had his home in the land where all the islands were born. They were all very high chiefs.

To Uli and Ku was born a very beautiful child whom they called Haka-lani-leo, the Listener-to-the-Heavenly Voice. As Haka-lani-leo grew older, she became the most beautiful woman of her time. Her skin was like the sun as it rises, or like the feathers of the *mamo*.

Haka-lani-leo married Ha'ka, King of Hilo, and to this union twelve sons were born. Eleven of these children possessed supernatural powers. Ten of them were ten feet tall. The eleventh son, Niheu, was much shorter than his brothers, being only five feet in height. Great wisdom was given to him. He could count even the hairs of his head.

These boys liked to test their strength by trying to lift a large ulua, ten fathoms and a yard long, that lived in the pond at Waiakea. Each boy would try to lift this fish to his shoulder. None succeeded but the small Niheu.

The twelfth and youngest son of Haka-lani-leo, Kana, came into the world in the form of a piece of rope and was at once thrown into the pig pen. The spirit of this child went to his grandmother, Uli, and begged her to save him. Uli departed at once for Hilo.

When the people saw her coming they called, "There comes the old woman, Uli. What brings her here? She has never come when her other grandsons were born."

As soon as Uli reached her daughter's home she asked, "Where is the little stranger that has come?"

"No stranger has come. We saw only a piece of rope which we threw into the pig pen," someone answered. "What do you want it for?"

Uli was led to the spot where the rope had been thrown. A pig was just about to devour this strange-looking object, but Uli picked it up and placed it in her calabash. When she reached her home she put the piece of rope into a calabash of water, saying, "It will never do if you come forth from the water with a pig's snout."

WILLIAM HYDE RICE

Uli watched the water closely and when she saw a snout appearing she quickly placed the rope in another calabash of water and soon a child appeared.

The happy grandmother placed the baby on the mats, and made a bower of maile, ieie and lehua branches to shade it from the sun. Then Uli went to work in her garden, which was very dear to her, and in which she was always busy.

About noon the grandmother returned and stopped the child's crying by food. So Uli cared for her youngest grandson for forty days. By that time he was forty fathoms long. As he grew in stature she enlarged the bower over him.

On the celebrated hill, Haupu, on the island of Molokai, lived Keoloewa, the king. With him were Pepee, Crooked-One, his general; Mo-i, High Chief, his *kahuna*; Moikeha, the High-Chief-who-Objects, his astrologer; and his three plover messengers, Kolea, or Plover; Ulili, or Sand-Piper; and Akekeke, or Snipe.

One day the king decided that he would marry, so he sent his bird messengers to find the most beautiful woman on earth, whose skin should be like the rising sun. The birds flew everywhere, looking for a woman who would answer the king's description. They found none until they had returned to Hilo and there they saw Haka-lani-leo, the most beautiful woman in the world, bathing in the sea by night.

At once the birds flew back to their king and told him that they had seen a woman whose skin was like the *o-o* and all the other beautiful birds of Hawaii.

Keoloewa decided that this wonderful woman should be his wife. He ordered a double canoe prepared for the journey. The birds flew ahead to show the way. They came to the harbor of Hilo just at dusk. There they waited patiently until the first cock crowed, and then they heard a sweet voice singing. The canoe was drifting in the water, where this beautiful woman usually rode the surf.

Just as Haka-lani-leo noticed the dark object, a voice called to her, "O beautiful woman, come here and rest before you ride the surf."

The woman swam to the canoe and getting into it was lost in admiration of its decorations which were made of the feathers of beautiful birds. It was not until the canoe was being rapidly paddled for Molokai, that she realized that she was being carried away. Then she began to mourn for her husband and her home at Hilo.

As the days passed and his wife did not return, Ha'ka sent his people to hunt on land and sea for her. She had disappeared completely. No one could find her.

Then the king called his eleven sons together and asked each one what he should do to find their beautiful mother. He came at last to Niheu who, absently stirring up the fire with a long stick, answered in these words: "The sea divides Hawaii from Molokai, where the wife you are weeping for is held a prisoner in the strong fortress of Haupa."

This answer made the king angry with Niheu whom he taunted because of his size. Niheu showed that even though he was small he was very strong. He jumped to the top of his house and, seizing the rafters, pulled the building down. Then he beat the ground with his stick and formed eight valleys with precipices so high that only the koue, the huge white tropic birds, could fly to their summits.

After he had done these things he said to his father, "Now you have seen what strength I have. But, alas, my strength is great only on this island. If my mother were on Hawaii I could get her for you, but she is on Molokai."

One day when Uli and her grandson, Kana, were working in their garden in the mountains they heard a great shouting coming from the seashore. Uli said that Kana's brothers were trying to lift the large ulua.

When Kana heard what his brothers were doing he was very anxious to test his strength with them. So he waited until his grandmother was busy, and then, after having shortened his body, he secretly hurried towards the spot where the boys were trying to lift the fish to their shoulders.

As he neared the pond of Waiakea, Kana asked the children why there was such a great noise. They replied that the chiefs were trying to lift the big fish, but only the smallest chief could do it.

Kana was greatly surprised that his tall brothers could not lift the fish, and said to the children, "Those men must be very weak if they can not lift that fish."

One of the children told the chiefs that an unknown boy was making fun strength. He was led before them and one of the brothers asked, "Did you say that we were weaklings because we could not carry this fish? Try to lift the fish yourself, if such strength belongs to you."

Kana at once jumped into the pond and turned the head of the fish towards the deep water. As the fish swam into the sea Kana held on

WILLIAM HYDE RICE

to its tail and was carried to Keahua and then back to the pond again. There he easily lifted the fish to his shoulder, and walked away with it.

When the astonished crowd saw this demonstration of strength, they cried, "This is the strongest boy of all."

These words angered the older chiefs, who felt that their strength had been ridiculed in the eyes of the people, for strength was possessed by those of high birth only, and to have a boy of unknown parentage surpass them was a great insult.

So Niheu cried that the boy was carrying the fish, belonging to the chiefs to his belau, where he would sacrifice it in gratitude for his strength.

In fact Kana's only thought was to carry his prize home to his grandmother. As he passed the heiau of Niheu, Kana was seized and carried into the heiau where he was tied to the main post. Leaving him there, his captors carried the fish back to the pond. It had been out of water so long that it was very weak.

As Uli was working in her fields, the thought came her that all was not well with her grandson, Kana. So, not finding him at home, she hurried to her other grandchildren.

When Nihen saw her he asked, "Do you know who that boy is, who tried to steal our fish? We have tied him up in the heiau for attempting to carry off the chiefs' fish."

Uli looked at the captive and at once saw that he was Kana. Turning to Niheu she replied, "That boy is no thief. He is your lord. You were born as a child. He was born as a piece of rope. That is the reason you did not know your brother."

Then Uli told Kana to walk. At once all his ropes fell off, and in his anger he began to tear down the heiau. Uli, fearing that the boy would entirely destroy the sacred place, ordered him to return with her to their mountain home.

As soon as the brothers had recovered from their surprise over the knowledge that Kana was living with their grandmother, Niheu told them that he was going into the mountains to build canoes with which to go to Molokai in search of his mother.

In the mountains he looked for timber suitable for his canoe. He soon found two wiliwili trees, seven feet in diameter.

The following day he felled these trees with two mighty strokes of his ax and commenced hewing them out. By evening he had almost finished them, so he decided to return in the morning.

Niheu was unable to sleep that night because he was very anxious about his canoes. As soon as daylight came, he hurried to the place where he was building them and was greatly astonished to find them standing up and growing again. He left them and looked for other trees suitable for canoes.

Having found two koa trees, Niheu cut them down with two strokes and, as on the previous day, almost finished the canoes by evening. Again he went home for the night.

At daylight he returned to the spot where he had left his unfinished canoes. He found these standing up and growing. The boy was very angry and muttered to himself, "This is the work of my grandmother, Uli. She wishes to bring my work to naught. She is a cruel woman to cast this spell upon me. I shall kill her."

For four days Nihen wandered here and there in the woods, hunting for Uli's home. At last Uli came upon him and asked: "Why have you wandered in the forest so long?"

Niken replied, "You will soon see why I am here. I am going to kill you now."

To these words of her grandson, Uli replied, "Is death the gift you bring to me? I have done you no wrong. Why did you not come to me and tell me that you needed canoes? I would have told you how to build them. It is not I, but your forefathers, the first builders of canoes, who are now in the netherworld, who will not allow you to fell the trees for canoes until they have been appeased. Kill me, if you wish, but then you will never be able to build canoes. Spare me, come home with me, and eat and drink. Then you shall go home and find a black pig without any white hairs. While you are gone, I shall prepare the *awa* root, the large calabash, and the grass to strain the *awa*. Thus with my help you can succeed."

These words appeased Niheu and he followed his grandmother into her house. While he was eating, he looked about for his newfound brother, Kana, but did not see him. As soon as he was refreshed, he hurried home and, finding the things Uli had mentioned, he brought them back and laid them at her feet. Then Uli told him to search in the forest until he found two lehua trees. After having felled and topped these, he should return to her.

Niheu followed his grandmother's instructions. Then she gave him the *awa* root and the black pig, which he carried to the place where the trees were lying. Having built an *imu* he killed and cooked the pig and prepared the *awa*. When all was ready Niheu called his ancestors to come and eat the food he had prepared for them. Then Niheu concealed him sell under the branches of the trees.

Soon he saw his strange-looking forefathers gathering around the table. After they had eaten the food one of their number, Kaikupakee by name, tried to put the tops of the trees onto the trees again. Niheu caught him and held him, saying that he was going to kill him. Kaikupakee answered that if he were killed Niheu's canoe would never be finished. So he was released and at once called out. "I will not build your canoes!"

Poor Niheu was very much discouraged, and hurried to his grandmother to tell her his troubles. Uli comforted the boy with these words: "Your canoes will be finished. Take this flag to the place where the trees lie, and with it mark out the size you wish the canoes to be."

Niheu did as Uli said, and then waited until darkness fell. Nothing was done to the trees that night, but the following night he heard voices saying, "Come, let us finish Niheu's canoes."

Then a wonderful thing happened. The canoes were instantly finished and a canoe house was built. After the ancestors had pulled the canoes under shelter they disappeared.

Early in the morning Niheu went to see what had been done and was greatly astonished to see everything finished. Happiness filled his heart. Looking for food, he came upon a house which he entered. There he saw several coils of rope. Niheu was very glad to see this rope for he needed it to pull his canoes to the sea. He also saw two sticks bent suitably for lashing his canoes together.

Just as Niheu was congratulating himself on his good luck the rope began to uncoil and Kana stood before his astonished brother, who was so frightened that he ran and jumped down a high *pali*. Kana stretched out his arms and rescued the falling boy. Bringing him back, he asked why he had jumped over the *pali*.

Nihen replied, "I jumped over that *pali* because I was anxious to see the handsome people who live down below. You caught me before I saw them."

To this falsehood Kana answered. "You are not speaking the truth. You ran because you saw my big eyes looking at you."

Niheu confessed this to be true. Then he hurried back to his grandmother and told her that the canoes had been finished as she had foretold. He asked her where the grandson lived, who had carried the ulua and whom she had called the lord of himself and his brothers, for that grandson must go to Molokai in search of his beautiful mother.

Uli at first did not want Niheu to take Kana away, but at last she consented, on condition that he be well treated.

Niheu found Kana and made known his errand. Kana consented to help his brother and explained the details of his plan. Niheu was to arrange his brothers and their followers in a long line extending from the mountains to the sea, with himself nearest the sea. These men must all be strong as the canoes were to slide down their shoulders to the sea.

When Kana saw that the long line of men was arranged he pushed the canoes with such force that they slid towards the sea like the wind, destroying everything in their way. The men tried to stop the canoes but were knocked down and killed.

As the canoes were sliding by Niheu, he caught hold of the man, the carved prows, and tried to stop them, but was unable to do so until he had been carried out to deep water. After he had anchored the canoes, he swam ashore and heard the great wailing over the sudden death of his older brothers.

Nihen hurried to Uli and Kana to tell them the sad news. Kana then told his brother to call the astrologer and the crews for the canoes. After everything was prepared, the people carried Kana to the sea.

Mo-i, the famous *kahuna* of Molokai, saw all these preparations to rescue Haka-lani-leo going on, on Hawaii. He called the plover and said, "Go to our lord, the king, and say that I have had a dream. If he wishes to escape harm he must return the woman he has stolen. If he refuses to do this, dire calamity will befall him. The crop of coconuts and taro will fail. *A-a*, small lava stones, will cover the land."

The plover flew to the entrance of the palace and made known to the king the dream of his *kahuna*. The king answered that no soldier was brave enough to come to Molokai and attempt to conquer her king.

Soon after, Mo-i slept and dreamed again. The plover, seeing his lips move, awakened him and asked why he was muttering in his sleep. Mo-i sent the plover to warn the king to send back the woman before the wards of Uli should come to rescue her, and to bring disaster to Molokai.

The king, in anger, sent his messenger to tell Mo-i to dream no more, or he would be punished.

Keoloewa then called his bodyguard of plovers, and told them to fly over the world to see if any soldiers were preparing for a trip to

Molokai. The plovers flew everywhere and, seeing no soldiers, all but one returned to the king. This one plover remained on Hawaii. He flew into the house of Uli. Then he went to Hilo and ran along the beach until he became thirsty. After he had gone to a stream for a drink, he flew back to the beach where he saw the tracks of a man in the sand. Each track was a fathom long and a yard wide.

With this information the plover returned to Molokai where he found that the king had built a big fire, to put to death the bird messengers because they had brought no news to him. When the king heard the report of the one plover who had stayed behind he put out the fire and spared the lives of the others. He believed that there was no strong man on Hawaii as the messengers had seen none.

In the meantime Mo-i dreamed again and as before sent the plover to the king with this message: "O King, return the woman within three days, or the war canoes will be seen approaching our island. In my dream I saw a figure flying above the fortress of Haupu. The head was higher than the mountain. The eyes were as bright as the evening star."

The king was very angry and ordered his soldiers to bring Mo-i before him. Then he sent for Moikeha, the sister of Mo-i, who could tell him if there was any truth in the words of her brother.

When Moikeha came before the king, he told her of the frequent warnings he had received from Mo-i. He said that he did not desire to return the beautiful woman he had stolen.

After hearing the king's message, Moikeha began her rites. She took a large calabash full of water and covered it with tapa. While she was doing this she heard the voice of Mo-i muttering: "Look well to what you are doing and you will see the big eyes of a man standing in the sea. He is coming for the woman who is held here without good cause. If he reaches the island, all will be destroyed. He is so tall that his head is higher than the fortress of Haupu."

As soon as Mo-i had ceased talking, his sister began to pray. While she prayed, a violent earthquake shook the land. When Moikeha removed the tapa from the calabash, she and Mo-i saw a pair of eyes as bright as the moon shining in the water. Then Moikeha knew that the dreams of her brother were true and she warned the king to return his captive to Hawaii.

The king would not listen to this advice and answered, "I will not return my prize. I am able to lift up my island until the fortress reaches the clouds. No man is tall enough to overlook it then."

Mo-i answered that the ward of Uli was able to become taller than any fortress. In fear, the people prepared for the day when the war canoes would reach their island. The king still listened not to the earnest entreaties of his generals and soldiers to return Haka-lani-leo, the beautiful woman of Hawaii.

Meanwhile, on Hawaii, Kana was making his preparations for the journey. He told Niheu to leave behind all the soldiers and paddlers, and to take with them only Pohaku, the Stone, a trusted companion. When all was prepared, the people wrapped Kana in mats, using one thousand of them to cover him. Then they placed him on the *pola*, the frame joining the double canoe.

As they put out to sea, the tide and the currents were against them. Many evil *akua* of the sea tried to delay them. The swordfish tried to destroy the canoe, but Pohaku lowered himself to the side of the canoe and the fish, striking against the stone of his body, was destroyed. This was the last of their troubles.

Soon they lay off Molokai. The people watching for war canoes were surprised to see a canoe with only one man paddling. A messenger was sent to ask if this was a war or a pleasure canoe. When Niheu answered that it was a war canoe, the king ordered war preparations to be carried out. In a short time the fortress was filled with soldiers ready to fight for their king.

In the meantime the canoe had landed, and Niheu had commenced to climb up the steep cliff by the aid of his long spear. The people believed that this small man was only a boy, but they wondered at the size of his spear.

Haka-lani-leo, safely guarded in the fortress, heard the words of the soldiers and, ordering them to stand aside, saw the man scaling the cliff and recognized her son, Niheu. Bitterly she wailed for the dear husband and strong sons from whom she had been torn.

The king gave his order to kill Niheu should he try to enter the fortress. But when the soldiers refused to allow him to enter, he struck them down with his spear. Then, using his spear as a bridge, he entered the fortress and rescued his mother. Placing her on his back, he crossed again on his spear and walked safely away.

As Mo-i saw the mother and her son going down the cliff, he called to the plover, "Anyone who is brave enough to pull some hairs from the head of Niheu can destroy his strength."

One of the plovers bravely descended the hill, and pulled five hairs from Niheu's head. Niheu stopped to count his hairs and, finding that five were gone, he cried out, "What slave has dared to steal some of my hair?"

In his anger Niheu dropped his mother and at once the soldiers seized her and carried her back to the fortress. Poor Niheu! He had lost both hair and mother! He was most unhappy. He sent his spear to find the person who had stolen his five precious hairs. It soon caught the plover and brought him, pinioned on its sharp point, to earth at Niheu's feet.

Niheu then rolled down the cliff, breaking his arm and injuring his leg. Weeping, he came to the canoe, and accused his brother of having sent him on this errand because he was small.

Kana was very angry, for he knew that now they would have a great deal of trouble in rescuing their mother again. Kana turned over in the mats and having thus broken the ropes, stood up. The king saw that this man was taller than his fortress, just as Mo-i had said. He ordered his turtles to raise the fortress. As Haupu was slowly raised higher and higher, Kana stretched his body, first his human body, then his rope body, next his convolvulus-vine body, his banana body, and last his spiderweb body.

When Niheu saw his brother in this strange form, he began to cry that he had been killed. He called out, "Kana, come down again to Uli."

Kana heard his brother's words and lowered his head into Hilo while his feet were still on Molokai. Uli knew that her grandchild was in some trouble, and she was very angry with Niheu, who had thought more of a few hairs of his head than of saving his beautiful mother.

Uli brought food to Kana. He ate all the food that was in the calabash. He ate all the food that was in the garden, taro, potatoes and bananas. As Kana took this nourishment his feet on Molokai began to grow. When Niheu saw the feet growing, he began to chop at them with a stone.

Kana called to his grandmother, "My feet are in pain. What is the trouble?"

Uli explained to him that Niheu was angry because he was hungry. So Kana promised to take him a hill of sweet potatoes.

Uli also explained to Kana that he must return to Molokai and break the backs of the turtles, so that they could not lift Haupu any higher.

Having heard these words Kana raised his head, and when the turtles tried to lift up the fortress he crushed them to death and pressed the mountain down to its original size. Niheu then climbed up and carried his mother down to the canoe.

The terrified people tried to escape but were driven over the *pali* by the big eyes of Kana. Only Mo-i and his sister escaped.

Kana cut Haupu off from the mainland. He gave the kingdom of Molokai to Hookekua, the king of Kekaha. Then he sent Nihen to Hawaii with his mother, and began his travels.

From Molokai Kana crossed to Oahu whence he soon went to Kipukai, on Kauai. There he saw the beautiful sisters of Kaneike. He traveled on until he reached Kalalau, where he frightened Kahuanui, Big-Foundations, who was making tapa, by stretching himself until his head reached the clouds.

Niihau was next visited by the traveler. After seeing the celebrated mat-weaver and the interesting points he stepped back to Kauai at a place called Ke'e, near Kalalau, which is called to this day, Kapuai-a-Kana, The Imprint-of-Kana's-Foot. Wherever Kana traveled on Kauai and Niihau he killed the *akua* who were destroying the people. At last Kana returned to Hawaii, where he found all the chiefs living happily. Nihen asked him to go around Hawaii with him. While they were staying in Kona, Niheu heard the people complaining because their king, Kahoalei, the Friend-of-the-Lei, made them cook food and fish for him. Niheu decided to talk with the king's messenger when he came with orders for the people, and so called to the man, but he ran away. Niheu followed and catching the poor fellow broke his back.

After this little adventure Niheu returned to Hilo. There his grand mother greeted him with these words: "You have been up to mischief. Your actions will bring trouble to us. Bring your brother to me before the calamity befalls us."

In the meantime Kahoalei had waited until midnight of the third night for the return of his messenger. At that hour the messenger crawled before his king, begging mercy and saying that he had been badly treated by the grandson of Uli.

Kahoalei was very angry and cried, "I shall punish Niheu. I shall take from Hawaii the sun, the moon, and the stars. Only where I am, shall there be light."

After Uli had sent Niheu to find Kana, she fastened a rope to the door of her house and then carried the rope to the sea, so that if the threatened darkness befell the land, she could find her way to and from the ocean. The people, seeing this, wondered what Uli was doing.

As soon as Niheu found his brother he started for Hilo with Kana on his back. They had gone only a short distance, when the sun was taken from the heavens and they had to feel their way. Kana then stretched his head about the clouds and so reached Uli's house.

"So you have come," said his grandmother. "I sent for you because I knew you were the only person who could recover the sun. Go now and find it. It is hidden under the earth. Before you go, see if there is any light in the sky. If there is, come and tell me."

Kana stretched his body until he reached the sky, where he found light. When he had reported this to Uli she said, "Take your brother with you and go up as far as your body will take you. The place that you will touch when you bend over will be Kahiki, and there you will find a spring. If anyone asks you your name, say 'I am yours and Uli's'"

With these instructions Kana started on his wonderful journey. When they reached the heavens, Niheu was chilled through and through, and so was left behind to die. Kana fell to Kahiki. The two old people there were startled by the noise of his fall, and each tried to make the other find what had fallen near them.

At last the old woman went out and seeing a white object in the spring tried to catch it with a stick. Failing to do this, she asked the object what it was and was surprised to hear it answer, "I am yours and Uli's."

Crying, "Oh my grandson!" the old woman carried Kana to her husband. They fed him until his strength returned and then asked him if he had come for the sun. When he replied that such was his errand, they gave him two guides who led the way. They sent a fire in front to show them the way and a wind behind to help them on.

When they reached the line dividing the kingdom from the land of the keepers of the spring, the guides left Kana, telling him to go wherever the wind directed.

So Kana journeyed on alone until he came to the guard, Manu-a, sitting by the king's door. Manu-a was friendly, and, urging the stranger to sit down by him, told him how he had to sit there, and watch the king and his followers eat and play while the cold rain fell upon him.

Kana was greatly interested. Soon he saw how the king got his food. He lifted a stone that covered a large hole in the sky and lowered his hand which was quickly filled with food by the people below.

While the king and his men were eating, the guard said to Kana, "Wait with me until they have finished. Then they will return the dishes and what remains of the food. Prop up the stone with your foot. They will think the hole is closed and will go back to their game. Then we may eat."

Kana did as he was told, and when they were alone he lowered his hand through the hole. As he did so the people saw a large black hand and they knew it was not the king's hand. Someone said, "This hand must belong to a soldier. No wonder it is fat. He sits and plays games all day while we labor for him. Perhaps even now he is demanding more food."

However, Kana's relatives recognized his hand, and filled it with food. Manu-a told him to drop the food. Then his hand was filled with water. This Kana also dropped. They next tried birds which the guard ordered up. These birds called out, "*Kiawea*," the call of the long-legged fish hawk, and the friends of the king thought that day had come. The king told them that there were no birds there.

Kana again lowered his hand, and it was filled with stars, which he threw into the heavens where they gave light. Then the moon was placed in his hand. Kana put it into the blue sky, where it remained giving light. He was next given all kinds of birds and fowl, and for the first time the rooster broke the morning stillness by crowing.

Yet again Kana lowered his hand through the magic hole in the sky. This time he was given the sun, which he placed in the sky, having received its solemn promise never to disappear again. Since that day no magic power has been able to deprive the people on earth of the great sun.

When the sun rose the king hurried out to see who was interfering with his powers. Kana was about to kill him, but was stopped by the king's promise to bring Niheu to life again.

As soon as Niheu was restored to life, Kana, accompanied by the king, stretched his body and returned to the house of Uli.

This was the king's first visit to this part of his kingdom, and so he planned to visit all parts of it. A canoe made of white chicken feathers carried him from place to place. So he traveled over the world for two years, conquering all lands. At the end of that time he returned to Hawaii and was deeply grieved to hear that the mighty Niheu and the artful Kana had died. He established his kingdom on the island of Hawaii, and collecting worthy ministers, ruled for many years.

WHEN KANA CAME FROM OAHU, wading through the sea, to Kipukai, Kauai, the turtles were raising up the hill of Haupu. Kana was afraid that it would reach too high, so he stretched himself up until his body was no larger than a spider's web. When he was tall enough, he put his foot on top of the mountain and crushed it down. So, now, three ridges run out from Haupu. He found his brother Niheu starving in Kipukai, and so he said he could relieve his brother's hunger. He lay down and stretched his body until his head reached the place where his grandmother was living on the hills back of Wahiawa. Then he called to his brother to cut his toe, and when Uli fed Kana *poi*, it ran through his body, and reached Kipukai, where Nihen sucked it out. Thus he saved his brother's life.

After Niheu had been fed, Kana found that his grandmother was making tapa, but the sun came up and went down so fast that there was no time for the tapa to dry. So Kana said he could make the days longer. He ordered all the people on the western side of the island to save all the coconut fiber and to braid it into ropes. When plenty of rope had been made, Kana stood on the top of the hill with the ropes coiled near him, and when the sun came up he lassoed it, and broke off some of the spokes. To this day, when the sun comes up, you can see that some of its spokes are shorter than the others, and those are the spokes which Kana broke. The sun then begged him to let it go. Kana said he would if the sun would promise to go slower, so as to make the days longer so that Uli would have time to dry her tapa. The sun agreed, and to this day has kept its promise. So we have to thank Kana for our long days.

KAILI-LAU-O-KEKOA

A Legend of Kauai

KAILI-LAU-O-KEKOA, THE-COVERING-OF-THE-KOA-LEAF, WAS THE ONLY daughter of Moikeha and Hooipo, two very high chiefs of Kauai. Her parents loved the child greatly, and gave her every care, engaging a nurse, or *kahu*, to be with her always. As Kaili-lau-o-kekoa grew, her beauty increased. After she had ridden the surf at Maka'iwa, near Waipouli, or had played *konane*, a complicated game resembling chess, her cheeks glowed like the rising sun.

One day, when her parents had gone to cultivate taro in Kapahi, Kaili-lau-o-kekoa was alone, playing *konane* with her nurse. Suddenly a strange man stood before the door. He asked the girl if she enjoyed *konane* very much. When she answered that she did, he suggested that she play a game with him. Kaili-lau-o-kekoa won the game by a score of nine to four. She said to the stranger, "You have been defeated by the daughter of Moikeha."

The man asked. "Is Moikeha still living?"

"Yes," answered Kaili-lau-o-kekoa. "He has gone to the taro patches now. Moikeha loves surf-riding and my mother. He will stay on Kauai till he dies."

After the stranger had heard these words, he said, "I believed that he was dead. I regret not being able to take him back to Molokai with me. When he returns, tell him that the high chief of Molokai has been here and has been defeated by Moikela's daughter in a game. Give your father and mother the aloha of Hea-kekoa."

When the chief from Molokai had spoken these words, he got into his canoe, and started for his island.

Now, at Pihanakalani, where all good things abounded—a legendary spot on Kauai above the Wailua river, that cannot be found nowadays—there lived two very high chiefs: Kaua-kahi-alii, The-Battle-of-the-Lone Chief, and his sister Ka-hale-lehua, The-House-of-Lehua. In this garden spot of Pihanakalani was the far-famed fountain of Wai-o-ke-ola, Water-of-Life, which could restore the dead to life, and renew the youth of the aged. Kana-kahi-alii owned a very loud-sounding flute called Kanika-wi, which could be heard as far away as Kapaa.

One night Kaili-lau-o-kekoa had been playing *konone* with her nurse until midnight. That night, while the girl slept, the nurse heard the flute crying, "Kaili-lau-o-kekoa, do you sleep?"

When the girl awoke in the morning her nurse told her the words she lad heard. Kaili-lau-o-kekoa was greatly excited and said, "Today we shall sleep all day so that I may be awake at midnight, for I must hear this voice from the hills when it calls me."

So they slept until evening. Then they played *konane* to keep themselves awake. At midnight they heard the flute voice calling, "Kaili-lau-o-kekoa, do you sleep in Puna? Is not the surf high?"

"I do not sleep. I shall search for you until I find you," answered the breathless Kaili-lau-o-kekoa.

Then she and her nurse started on their search. They climbed up the mountain side and at daylight reached Kuamoo.

When the sister of the flute player saw these two women coming, she sent the heavy mist and the blinding rain to delay their journey. They found shelter in a hollow tree and when the rain had ceased they went on. Kaili-lau-o-kekoa soon saw a house where a bright fire was burning.

As the two women approached the house of Ka-hale-lehua, the sister of the flute player, she took pity on them, and welcomed them. She took off their wet clothes, and gave them each a dry *pa-u*. Then she prepared a meal for her unbidden guests. She placed before them a platter of *limu lipoa*, choice seaweed, and little striped manini fish, still alive. Kaili-lan-o-kekoa was greatly surprised to see the live fish, and said to her nurse. "We live near the sea yet we never have live fish. This place is far from the sea. How is it that the fish are still alive?"

Her hostess answered her by saying that she and her brother had a fish pond near their house.

After the meal was finished Kaili-lau-o-kekoa went in search of the flute that had called her away from home. She came to the room of Kana-kahi-alii and found the flute hidden in his breast. At once a great love for this chief filled the heart of the girl, and she forgot her fond parents and stayed with him.

When the parents of Kaili-lau-o-kekoa fomd that their daughter was gone, they began to search for her. At last they came to the house where she was living with the young chief, and carried them both to Kapaa. There they tied the chief to a post in a house.

The first day he was given nothing to eat. On the second day a boy passed by, and, seeing the prisoner, asked if he had been given any food or water. When he heard that he had received none, he returned to his parents and made known to them the chief's condition. They ordered their son to put water in a coconut shell, and to get another one for food, so that he could throw them to the prisoner. With these he crawled through the rushes so that no one would see him.

The boy carried out his parents' instructions on that day, and on many following days. The chief began to look well again.

When the father of Kaili-lau-o-kekoa had recovered from his anger he called his daughter to him and asked her to explain how she came to be in the mountains. She told him that she had heard the flute calling to her, and had wanted to make of the man who played it either a husband or a friend.

Her parents decided to allow the *kahuna* to settle the matter. When they were called together, and had heard the story they all agreed that Kaili-lau-o-kekoa should marry the chief if he could give his genealogy. As soon as Kaua-kahi-alii was called before them, he proved that he was a very high chief, and so the beautiful chiefess was given to him in marriage. The boy who had carried food and water to the chief in prison became his great friend and was made luna, or head man, over all his lands.

The Rain Heiau

A Legend of Molokai

ON MOLOKAI THERE IS AN interesting heiau,[4] called Ka-imu-kalua-ua. In a little cave opposite lived the woman Pauulea. Nearby her two brothers Kaoliu and Mawe lived in the form of hills.

Pauulea made tapa in the cave and spread it out to dry. As soon as she has spread it in the sun her brothers would send rain to wet the tapa and tease her.

This happened many times and at last Pauulea found a way out of her difficulty. Taking small oblong stones, she built a heiau. As the rain fell she caught the drops in the stones and cooked them. Thus she always had fair weather to dry her tapa.

---

4. This heiau is situated on the edge of a little valley, about a mile northwest of the place where Mr. George Cooke now lives. Mr. Cooke has enclosed it with a fence, so that none of the stones will be removed.

Puu Ka Mo-o

How Lizards Came to Molokai

IN ONE OF THE VALLEYS of Molokai lived the most beautiful woman of the island. It happened that every night she was visited by a man who always left before daylight so that she was not able to discover who he was. This suspense began to tell on her and she slowly wasted away.

In their anxiety her parents summoned a *kahuna* to see if he could tell the cause of their daughter's ill health. He made known the girl's secret and said that during the day this nightly visitor was a *mo-o*, or monster lizard; only at night could he take a human form.

The *kahuna* arranged this plan to destroy the girl's tormentor. He was to hide in the house where the girl slept. The girl was to keep her visitor awake as long as possible, so that when he slept he would sleep soundly. Then when deep sleep held him the *kahuna* would tie white tapa rags to his back. At daylight the man would be turned into a *mo-o*, and crawl off, through the bushes, leaving his trail marked by white tapa rags.

This plan was carried out. The *kahuna* and his men followed the trail of the *mo-o* until they came to a rocky hill still known as Puu ka Mo-o[5]. There, surrounded by stones, they saw the monster lying in the sun fast asleep. All the people were ordered to collect wood. This was placed around the *mo-o* and set afire. As the heat of the fire burned the body of the *mo-o*, it burst open and myriads of small *mo-o* were thrown out and ran away among the bushes.

Thus was the beautiful girl saved from her nightly visitor, and thus were the little worm-like lizards introduced into the islands. The hill is still known as Puu ka Mo-o, the Hill-of-the-Monster-Lizard.

---

5. Puu ka Mo-o is situated about a mile and a quarter northwest of Mr. George Cooke's home, Kauluwai.

WILLIAM HYDE RICE

MANO-NIHO-KAHI

A Legend of Oahu

NEAR THE WATER HOLE IN Malae-kahana, between Laie and Kahuku, lived a man called Mano-niho-kahi, who was possessed of the power to turn himself into a shark. Mano-niho-kahi appeared as other men except that he always wore a tapa cloth which concealed the shark's mouth in his back.

Whenever he saw women going to the sea to fish or to get *limu* he would call out, "Are you going into the sea to fish?"

Upon hearing that they were, he would hasten in a roundabout way to reach the sea, where he would come upon them and, biting them with his one shark's tooth, kill them.

This happened many times. Many women were killed by Mano-niho-kahi. At last the chief of the region became alarmed and ordered all the people to gather together on the plain. Standing with his *kahuna*, the chief commanded all the people to disrobe. All obeyed but Mano-niho-kahi, Shark-with-One-Tooth. So his tapa was dragged off and there on his back was seen the shark's mouth. He was put to death at once and there were no more deaths among the women.

Laniloa, The Mo-o

A Legend of Oahu

Laniloa is the name given to a point of land which extends into the ocean from Laie. In ancient times this point was a *mo-o*, standing upright, ready to kill the passerby.

After Kana and his brother had rescued their mother from Molokai and had taken her back to Hawaii, Kana set out on a journey around the islands to kill all the *mo-o*. In due time he reached Laie, where the *mo-o* was killing many people. Kana had no difficulty in destroying this monster. Taking its head, he cut it into five pieces and threw them into the sea, where they can be seen today as the five small islands lying off Malae-kahana: Malualal, Keauakaluapaas, Pulemoku, Mokuaaniwa, and Kilewamoku.

At the spot where Kana severed the head of the *mo-o* is a deep hole which even to this day has never been fathomed.

Manuwahi

A Legend of Oahu

At Laie lived Manuwahi, Free Gift, with his son, Ka-haku-loa, The-Lord-of-a-Long-Land; his grandson, Kaiawa, Bitter Sea, and his great grandson, Kauhale-kua, The-Village-on-the-Ridge. These men were the keepers of the *akua* at Laie. Manuwahi and his children were hairless and were possessed of supernatural powers.

Manuwahi planted black and white awa far up in the mountains for the of the *akua*. Every *awa* root planted was given one of these names, Kalaka, The-Hole-That-Gives-a-Shadow; Kumumu, Blunt-Edged; Kahiawa, Best-Awa, or Kumilipo, The Root-of-Unconsciousness. This was done so that Manuwahi, when sending one of his sons for a piece of awa could designate the exact one he wished.

When the *awa* was given to him, Manuwahi would prepare it, and then summon the *akua* from the North, South, East, and West, as well as from above and below, to drink of it. They prayed in this wise, before they drank:

> *Gods of the Morning, Gods of the Night,*
> *Look at your progeny:*
> *Grant them health, Grant them long life;*
> ***Amama ua noa**—it is free!*

It happened that during this time, Kamehameha I had come to conquer Oahu. He had succeeded in subduing all the island except Malae-kahana, between Laie and Kahuku. Determined to add this place to his conquests, the king sent one of his bodyguard, Ka-hala-iu, In-the-Shadow-of-the Hala-Tree, with many of his bravest soldiers to subdue Malae-kahana.

Ka-hala-iu marched as far as Hanapepe the first day, where he spent the night. Early the next morning he set out and meeting Manuwahi, whom he did not recognize, asked him where the powerful *kahuna* of Malae-kahana lived.

Manuwahi answered, "Pass over the river and you will see a spring and nearby a hut with trees about it. This is his home."

Ka-hala-iu did as he was told and had soon surrounded the hut with his soldiers. When Manuwahi's son came out Ka-hala-iu asked him, "Where is your father?"

"Did you meet a bald-headed man?" asked the boy in turn.

"Yes," replied Ka-hala-iu.

"Well, that was my father. Why did you come here?"

"I came to kill your father by the orders of King Kamehameha," answered the King's man. Deciding it would profit them nothing to kill the son, the soldiers departed for Hanapepe by the *makai* side of the hill, and failed to meet Manuwahi, who had returned to his home by the *mauka* side.

The next morning the King's bodyguard again surrounded with his soldiers the home of the *kahuna*. Manuwahi came out and asked, "What are you here for? Did you come for battle?"

"Yes," answered the fearless soldier, "we came to kill you."

Whereupon Manuwahi called to his assistance all the *akua* from the North, South, East and West as well as those from above and below. They came at once and gave battle to the soldiers of the king. The *akua* fought by biting and scratching their assailants and before long they had killed all but Ka-hala-iu.

Ka-hala-iu cried out, "Spare my life, kahuna of the gods, and I will stay with you."

"What can you do if you stay with me?" asked Manuwahi.

"I will plant *awa* for you. I came from Hawaii, where I lived by planting *awa*," answered Ka-hala-iu.

But Manuwahi said, "I do not need you. Go back and tell your king that even his bravest soldiers were not able to conquer Malae-kahana Tell him that all but you were killed by the *akua* there."

When Kamehameha had heard these words he sent Ka-hala-iu back with another body of soldiers with orders that he must conquer Malae-kahana.

In the meantime, Manuwahi had moved with his sons up to the cave of Kaukana-leau, where the natives made their stone adzes. There the King's soldiers met them. As before, Manuwahi called all the *akua* to his aid. Again the soldiers were quickly put to death and only Ka-hala-iu was left. So Malae-kahana was not conquered.

Ka-hala-iu respected and admired Manuwahi so much that he was very anxious to remain with him, and so he asked again to be allowed to remain as an *awa* grower. Manuwahi consented this time and gave him one side of the valley to cultivate in *awa*.

One day as Ka-hala-iu was preparing the side hill for its cultivation, he noticed that on the opposite side of the valley, trees and bushes were falling in every direction, as if a whirlwind were uprooting them. This frightened him very much, as he could not understand the phenomenon, so he ran in great haste to Manuwahi, and asked what it meant. Manuwahi told him that his *akua* were helping in the clearing of the side hill, and that if he wished them to help him, they would gladly do so. Ka-hala-iu was only too happy to have help, so he called upon the *akua*, and in a short time both sides of the valley were cleared, and were growing luxuriantly with the most beautiful *awa*.

After the battle, between Ka-hala-iu and the *akua* for the possession of Malae-kahana, Manu-ka, Frightener of Birds, one of Manuwahi's sons, moved to Kaneohe, where he died sometime later. He was buried *makai* of the present road. The natives dug a very large grave, but before they could cover the body, the *akua* brought red dirt from Ewa, in a cloud, which filled the grave, and made a red hill above it, which can be seen to this day. There is no other red dirt in that district.

MAKUAKAUMANA

A Legend of Oahu

*The story of a man who was swallowed by the big fish,
and of this man's gods, Kane and Kanaloa.*

MAKUAKAUMANA WAS A FARMER, PLANTING *AWA*, bananas, and sugar cane for his gods, and taro and sweet potatoes for himself and his friends. He and his wife lived at Kauluanui in the district of Koolau, on Oahu. They had one child, a boy, and when this boy was twelve years old his mother died.

After the death of his wife, Makuakaumana went alone to his farm in the mountains, leaving his son in charge of his house. Whenever Makua ate, or slept, or worked, he prayed to his gods, Kane and Kanaloa, but he did not know exactly how to end his prayers, for he always omitted the words *"amama ua noa."*[6]

The gods had noticed Makua's strict observance of prayer and so they had decided to take him to live with them on Ulukoa, the land that was hidden from the sight of man, and called the Island-Hidden-by-Kane. The people who lived on this island were the direct descendants of Kane. They were O-Kane, Kanaloa, Kane-of-the-Water-of-Life, Kane-of-Thunder, Kane-that-Breaks-the-Heaven, Kane-of-the-Rocks, Kane-of-the-Rolling-Thunder, Kane-of-the-Rough-Cave, Kane-of-the-White-Cave, Kane that-Sleeps-in-the-Road, Kane-that-Sleeps-in-the-Water, Kane-that-Shakes the-Earth, Kane-of-the-Light, Kane-in-the-Break-of-Day, Kane-in-the-Twilight, Kane-in-the-Whirlwind, Kane-in-the-Sun, Kane-in-the-Prayers, Kane-the-Skilfull, Kane-the-Jumper, Kane-the-Brave-One, Kane-Who-Hid-the-Island, Kane-the-Watchman, Kane-that-Ran-on-the-Cliff, and Kane-the Eyeball-of-the-Sun.

Each of these gods had his own tasks to perform as indicated by his name. These gods lived in bodies of men on the beautiful land of Ulukoa. There all food grew without cultivation. There everyone was happy. There no weeping, no wailing, no pain, no sickness, no death was known. There the inhabitants lived forever and when they became very

---

6. "Amama ua noa," "The prayer is finished, or freed." This is almost equivalent to "Amen," but its use antedates any Christian influence.

WILLIAM HYDE RICE

old, their bodies were changed into spirit bodies without tasting of death, and then they become gods and lived in the clouds. From their home in the clouds their spirits could come to earth in men's bodies or in spirit bodies as they preferred.

It happened that a great fish had come ashore in the bay of Kahana, Koolan, near the village. His body was covered with stones on which grew *opihi* shells and many varieties of *limu*. The people were walking on his body.

As Makua was working alone on his farm, two men ran to him and asked. "Why do you keep on working in your garden? Do you not know that a big fish has come ashore at Kahana and that all the people are hurrying to see it?"

Makua noticed that these men were carrying staffs. He inquired whence they had come and how they had heard of the big fish.

They replied that they had come from Kahana.

Then Makua said, "You must be very spry to come so quickly such a great distance. How did you know my name? You are strangers to me. I have never seen you before."

The strangers answered that the people in the village had told them his name, saying that he was the only one to cultivate anything in the mountains and that they were looking for *awa*, bananas, and sugar cane, for which things they were longing greatly.

Makua said, "I have plenty of awe, bananas, and sugar cane, but I have planted all these things for my gods, Kane and Kanaloa."

Hearing these words, the strangers winked at each other and asked, "Have you ever seen your gods?"

"No," replied Makua, "I have never seen them, but I am told that they are very kind-hearted and full of love for anyone that worships them. That is why I have chosen them for my gods and planted these things for them."

"If anyone besides your gods eats these things, what will become of him?" asked the strangers.

"No one will come and take the things that I have planted for the gods. It is not the right of anyone," replied Makua.

"But, suppose you will allow anyone to eat of the food you have planted for your gods, how then can trouble be avoided?" continued the strangers.

"By praying to my gods," Makua answered.

"How shall they pray?" inquired the strangers.

"Thus," said Makia:

> *"O, Kane, O, Kanaloa,*
> *Here is the taro, the banana,*
> *Here the sugar cane, the **awa**,*
> *See, we are eating it now."*

Then the strangers laughed and said, "Such a short prayer will not tire you much. It is only a few words."

"Yes," said Makua, "my prayer is short. No one has taught me how to pray, so that I can make a longer prayer. But I think my gods accept my prayers. If they do not accept them because they are short, that is no excuse for me to cease praying. As long as I live I shall pray to my gods. I am now halfway through my life, and I have prayed at all times. Should I stop now, all my prayers would be lost, and I should receive no blessing from my gods."

"What blessing do you expect to receive from your gods for your devotion?" asked the strangers.

"I shall have enough to eat. All things will grow well on my farm without too much hard work. All that I plant will bear abundantly for my gods, and they in turn will grant me long life," said Makua.

"Then why did your wife die, if the gods have power to grant long life?" persisted the strangers.

Hearing this question, Makua hung his head and tears dropped from his eyes as he answered, "Because my wife died, one cannot say that the gods have no power to grant long life. All men must go by the same path, all from the old man to the child that cannot even creep."

When the strangers heard this answer, they said, "You will not be disappointed in the blessing you hope to receive from your gods, for we see that you have great faith. Now prepare banana, *awa* and sugar cane for us. Before we eat, pray to your gods so that we may hear your prayer and commit it to memory, and so learn to worship your gods."

Makua was filled with joy to think that these men wanted to worship his gods. So he quickly prepared the food, and as he placed it before them, he prayed thus:

> *O Kane and Kanaloa,*
> *I am eating with my strangers*
> *The banana and the sugar cane.*

　　　　　　　　　　　　　　　WILLIAM HYDE RICE

As the men ate, Makua asked them what they thought of his prayer.

They replied, "There is nothing amiss in your prayer, for we know your great faith and your good works. We believe your gods will approve of your prayer as we do. What would be gained by our changing the language of your prayer?"

The strangers said that they must depart. One presented Makua with a staff, saying, "This staff I received from my ancestors. It is a great help in the cultivation of land. Dig a hole with it and place a plant in the hole and it will grow very fast. A potato will grow so large that no one will be able to carry it."

The other stranger said, "Here is my present to you. This staff is an heirloom from my ancestors. Its great property is to carry loads, lessening their weight. You can carry with it many rows of potatoes without feeling their weight in the least. But I warn you that when you go to the sea to bathe, you should tell your son the uses and values of these staffs, so that when you are absent he will care for them, and then your gods will never lack for food. Your son will never grow tired at work and will never be hungry."

Makua seemed very doubtful about the truth of these wonderful words. He said, "You seem to have the bodies of men. Where have you received the power to endow these staffs with the supernatural powers you say they possess?"

One man replied, "You are right. We have no power. The power came from our ancestors. Now to dispel your doubts about the properties of the staffs, go, and with the digging stick, dig up all the *awa* in the fields in front of you. Into each hole throw a slip of *awa*."

Makua quickly did as he was told. The *awa* came from its hole as though it were thrown from the ground. Makua could feel no resistance as he dug. He kept on digging and planting until half of the field was finished and he felt no weariness.

Then Makua began to wonder how he could carry so many bundles of *awa*, for one bundle was all he had been able to lift. He decided that it would take four hundred people to carry all he had dug with this wonderful staff.

But the stranger urged him to keep on, saying, "How will you know the value of the stick? Keep on until you have dug up the whole field or I shall take the staff from you and you will only have been helped in the planting of the *awa*."

So Makua finished the whole field. Then the strangers pulled off from the fence much *kowali* or convolvulus plant and told Makua to throw it over the *awa*. Makua did as he was told, throwing the vine over the *awa* root and when he had reached the other side of the field he noticed that the vine had grown over the *awa* and had gathered it all into two big piles. Makua was amazed at this and as he stood looking at the piles and thinking that the men had done the work, one called out to him, "Come and get my lifting stick and see if my gift is of any value."

Makua took the staff with grave doubts. He felt it could not lift so great a burden. But he placed the ends of the stick in the piles of *awa*. As he straightened himself to lift the load, he felt only the weight of the staff,—none of the weight of the *awa*. Then he began to walk toward the sea, but his feet hardly touched the earth and he felt almost as if he were flying. So he lost sight of his guests and in a very short time he found that he was near his home by the sea. As he lowered his bundle to the ground, he saw again his two friends who asked what he thought of their gifts.

Makua replied, "These staffs will be my parents. I came here as a bird flies, feeling no weight and with great speed. Usually darkness falls before I reach my home. Now it is still daylight. I thank you, and have no longer any doubts as to their usefulness."

The man who had given Makua the digging stick said, "You will not see the real value of my gift until tomorrow when you return to your farm. I warn you to care for these sticks most diligently, but do not injure others through their power or take others' property. You must observe the laws of these sticks. If you do wrong with them, they will lose their magic properties and you will return to your life of hard labor. But if you do as I say, these staffs will retain their power and you may bequeath them to your descendants who in turn must care for them and do no injury to them and they too will receive a blessing from them."

Then the strangers said that they must depart, but Makua urged them to tarry until they had eaten. They replied that they would stay longer when they came again, for then he would have the means of entertaining strangers without trouble. So saying, they disappeared behind the house. Makua followed, hoping to see in what direction they went, but they were nowhere to be seen and he wondered about their supernatural disappearance.

Now these strangers were Makua's gods, Kane, who had presented the *o-o*, or digging stick, and Kanaloa, who had presented the *auamo*, or lifting stick. They had come because they had noticed Makua's weariness after his hard work and also because they wanted to try his faith, after the death of his wife.

Calling his son to him, Makua explained the power of the sticks and the care which must be taken of them. He said that on the following day they would go to the farm, and the boy should see how well he could use them. Food enough for forty men to carry would be prepared and the boy should carry it with the magic staff. This pleased the boy, for he thought that men would wonder at his great strength.

So they ate their evening meal and retired to rest, Makua first offering prayers to his gods At daybreak, they hurried to the farm, where they were astonished to see that in each hole where the *awa* had been planted the previous day three big bunches were growing.

Then Makua realized for the first time that his visitors were not men and he cried out, "The men who came were not strangers. They must have been my gods. No man would have had power to do these things. The strangers are none other than my gods!"

So saying, he thanked his gods for having revealed themselves to him and then quickly set to work. He gave the *o-o* stick to his son, telling him dig in all the fields for all the food plants. In a short time the food was thrown into bundles and was covered with the *kowali* vine which quickly tied the food into two larger bundles. Taking the *auamo* stick and placing its ends under the bundles, the boy lifted them as easily as his father had done, feeling no weight. Makua laughed with joy and said, "This is the life which my gods have granted to us, in return for my faith in them and care of them."

So father and son turned towards their home. In a short time the boy with his big load was far ahead of his father, who tried to overtake him, but could not, and the boy reached home before Makua was halfway.

Reaching home, Makua as usual prepared his meal and also a meal for his gods. Then he saw two very old men approaching and he invited them to eat with him. Makua asked these men if they had any gods and they replied that they had Kane-huli, or Seeking-Kane; Kane-puaa, Hog-Kane; Hina-puku-ai, Hina-Gatherer-of-Food; and Hina-puku-ia, Hina-Gatherer of-Fish.

This number of gods surprised Makua and he inquired why they had so many gods. The old men promised to explain after they had eaten and then Makua prayed thus, "O Kane, O Kanaloa, hear. My son, my guests, and I will eat bananas and sugar cane, things you like."

"Your prayer is not right," said the old men. "We must first pray correctly and then we shall eat. This food has been prepared for your gods. They must first eat or some dire disaster will befall you and your son. No harm will come to us as we are only strangers here."

These words made Makua very angry because he thought that these old men did not have faith in his gods, so he decided to kill them. They could see what was passing in his mind, and when he tried to lay hold of them, they called out, "Do not touch us, for we are old men without strength who have only a few more days to live. Your gods do not like to have their followers shed blood."

Makua was filled with fear and prayed, "O Kane and Kanaloa, I have sinned in thinking to break your laws. May the old men forgive me and teach me to pray."

The men forgave Makua and taught him this prayer:

O Kane and Kanaloa,
*Here is the **awa** for You,*
Here is the sugar cane,
Here is the banana
We shall eat and drink by Your power.
You give life to me. Do not shorten this life.
Grant me the life which does not wane,
And You shall have the kapu.

Then they drank the three cups of ana and they ate the food which Makua had prepared and explained that their gods were Kane-huli-honua, the Giver-of-Great-Lands; Kane-puaa, the God-of-Sacrifices; Hina-puku-ai, who granted sufficient food; and Hina-puku-ia, who supplied the food from the sea.

"You must worship your gods not only by prayer, but also by sacrifices," they said. "When offering food, ask Hina-puku-ai to carry it to your gods, Kane and Kanaloa. If you are offering fish, call upon Hina-puku-ia, for to her belongs the power over the fish."

Makua was very happy to learn from these old men that he should worship his gods by sacrifices, for he had not known this before, and the knowledge gave him new life.

The men told him that there were many more useful things he should add to his worship which they could not teach him, but someone might come in the future who could teach him more.

WILLIAM HYDE RICE

Then they prepared to depart, and as night was at hand Makua urged them to stay until morning, but they said that they must hurry on to see the strange fish which had come to land. Makua asked if this fish was good to eat and they said they did not know, as they had not seen it and had only heard of it through others.

So these old men departed. They were very high gods, Kane-huli-honua and Kane-puaa, and they had come to teach Makua the proper way to pray and to sacrifice. They also wished to interest Makua in the great fish.

When Makua awoke the next day, he told his son to remain at home while he went to Kahana to see the big fish he had heard of. As he came near the fish, he saw a great crowd about it. They all thought it was dead. A man explained that the stone *pali*, or cliff, extending to the sea was the fish. When it had come ashore, its tail and its back had been seen, but now it was covered with sand and looked like a *pali*.

While Makua was looking at it, he heard a great noise and saw a great crowd of men and women covered with leis coming to see the fish. When they reached it, they climbed upon its back and jumped from it into the water. They had been to see the fish before and had now returned to dive from it, covered with leis as their custom was. They were enjoying it greatly, as the fish gave them their first opportunity to dive, for up to this time there had been no cliffs on their shore.

Seeing the grand time his friends were having, Makua decided to hurry home to prepare himself for diving.

At home he found his son looking very happy because he had been to the farm and had found that everything which had been planted with the stick had grown rapidly and was ready to be harvested. The sugar cane had grown so high, it had fallen over and had grown up again.

Makua told his son not to be surprised at such blessings, for they would receive them continually, if they followed the gods' instructions. Then he explained all the gods had told him about the use and care of the sticks. The boy promised to follow these instructions and Makua was very much pleased, saying, "Blessings will follow you, my son. You will not die, nor yet grow old."

Makua was anxious to see for himself how the farm looked, so he forgot for the time being about the fish, and went to the farm. There standing by his door, he saw two very strange and beautiful men. No one in Koolau could equal them. One held a *malo-pua-kai*, the red-dyed loin-cloth for surfing, the other a *kuina-kapa-papa'u*, the thick bedcovering of many colors. Makua gave them his aloha, yet he was filled with fear, for he thought that they must be great chiefs from the island of Hawaii, for they wore the cloaks of beautiful feathers from Hawaii. Makua feared that he would make mistakes in their presence. The strangers saw all that was passing in his mind.

Makua had thought that he would always be able to recognize his gods, having seen them once, but he did not know them now and took them for chiefs.

The men asked for food. Makua told his son to bring the awa. He quickly got it from the pile and prepared three cups of it as he was very skillful. He also prepared three joints of cane and three bananas.

When Makua saw these things being prepared which belonged to his gods, he cried out, "Did you pray to our gods?"

"No, I did not," answered the boy, "because I am very hungry. Not since the day of my birth have I so longed for food."

"As a punishment for this crime I must put you to death, and sacrifice you to my gods, or the penalty will fall on me," sadly replied Makua.

He began to prepare a big fire for the sacrifice. Meanwhile, the strangers were watching and gave the boy power to speak,

He asked. "Will you kill me in that fire?"

"No. I shall kill you first by means of a stone adz, and then when you are dead, I shall throw you into the fire!"

The boy cried out with a loud voice, and the stranger with the wing kapa, who was Kanaloa, gave power to him to resist his father and he asked, "In whose name will you kill me, and to whom will you sacrifice me?"

Makua replied, "I shall kill you in the name of Hina-puku-ia, and I shall sacrifice you to Kane and Kanaloa."

The boy stood before his father, saying, "Aloha, will you look at my body? What part of it is like a fish, or like food, that you sacrifice me to Hina-puku-ia and Hina-puku-ai? Neither has power over the body of man."

These words troubled Makua, for he knew that his son was right, and that he should not kill him nor throw him into the fire in the name of the Hina. So he decided to do it without calling on them, for he was angry that his son had disobeyed him. He tied the boy with a rope.

The strangers, seeing the boy tied, gave him power to call out, so that his father would have compassion on him, "O Mother! I am to be burned today in the fire, and shall go into your presence with a body burned by fire. Why did not my father kill me while I was yet small? He has allowed me to grow up, and now wishes to slay me. O Mother! Come and rescue me. I am bound up. I shall be killed with an adz, and shall be thrown into the fire. I shall die today."

These words caused Makua to weep. He could not longer conceal his love for his son because the boy's prayers had recalled fond memories. He kissed his son and said, "Alas, my son, I cannot refuse to do what I have promised the gods in return for their wonderful gifts."

So saying, he placed the boy on the ground and taking his stone adz, prayed, "I am fulfilling my promise to you by sacrificing my only son. Receive this sacrifice, and grant me in turn life which shall never cease."

Having finished this prayer, Makua struck at his son with the adz, but he could not strike him. Three times he missed his aim, the adz falling to the ground each time. Failing to kill the boy, Makua untied him and hurled his body against a great stone. Three times he did this and each time the boy was unharmed, having no mark even upon his body.

As the angry father seized him the fourth time, Kane called out, "Makua, stop! Do not touch the boy again. Your gods will pardon your sin. There is a law among your gods that if a man tries three times to keep his promise and fails, the sin will no longer be held against him. But if he tries the fourth time, then the sin will be his own. So we command you to take your child into the house and, before we eat, pray to your gods for a blessing on this food, and thank them for not allowing you to kill your only son."

These words were like a calabash of cool water poured over Makua's head. They cooled all his troubled thoughts and took away the desire to kill his son. He knew that the stranger spoke the truth and, taking his son into the house, he said, "Aloha, my boy, you shall live. I have forgotten my desire to kill you. I know that I am forgiven by my gods."

Then Makua prepared the food and as his guests sat down before it, he prayed as the old men had taught him. Kanaloa teasingly asked who had taught him to pray, and told him that his prayers were good. He said the gods would try his faithfulness to them three times.

Makua asked why he was to be tried three times and Kanaloa replied, "Because there are three worlds where men who worship the gods will live. First, this world that we are living on; second, the world hidden from the eyes of man, belonging to Kane-huna-moku, Hider-of-the-Island; third, the world where Kane lives and where he takes men good enough to become gods."

"Where do bad people go?" asked Makua.

"First, such people go to a world where men have done neither good nor evil and where they wait to be rescued; second, to the world where they see joy and sorrow; third, to the world where they shall weep because of the heat which lasts day and night," explained Kanaloa.

"In what bodies shall men pass to these worlds?" inquired Makua.

"In spirit bodies," answered Kane.

Makua realized that he would be tried three times. We have seen him tried twice—first, on his farm, then in suffering the sacrifice of his son. There is yet one trial for him to endure.

As the strangers left the house, one gave his *malo-pua-kai* to Makua, saying, "This is my gift to you for your entertainment. Its value is that it shall make you invisible to the eyes of man."

The other gave Makua his sleeping tapa, saying, "This is my gift to you. Its value is that it shall take away from your body the heat of the sun."

Makua was very happy to have received these new gifts. He said, "This is the third time that I have entertained strangers. First, my gods. Then, the old men who taught me how to pray and sacrifice to my gods. Now these handsome men with the *kapu* of the chief."

Now Makua lost all interest in going to his farm to work. He did not have to plant as everything grew luxuriantly. He had plenty of taro, sugar cane, and bananas. He told his son that their days of hard labor were over, life would henceforth be easy for them. And so Makua decided to go again to see the big fish. He tied the *malo* around his waist and placed the tapa over his shoulders. As he kissed his son farewell, the boy began to weep, saying, "I feel that you will not come back. Fear takes hold of me. I fear this trip will separate us. Something is about to befall you."

The father reassured the boy with these words, "Fear not. We are not men without gods. You have seen with your own eyes that our gods have visited us. Have they not given us gifts? Be cheerful and await my return."

The boy dried his tears and put away fear.

Makua hurried to Kahana. There the people were gathered and they were greatly surprised to see him wearing a *malo* and tapa. They asked him if he were cold. He replied that these were gifts from his gods who had come to his house a few days before. So the men all made *malo* and tapas for themselves and from that day began to wear them.

Then they asked Makua why he had come and he said that he might jump off the stone *pali* of the fish into the sea. They thought he would ruin his beautiful gifts in the water, but Makua said that he would swim without them.

Then the people asked him to wait until the next day, so that they could all join him. He consented and rested and feasted that day.

The next day they all climbed along the back of the fish as they supposed it to be dead. Makua saw many *opihi*, or mussels, clinging to the stones on the fish's back. He began to break the *opihi* off with a stone. He forgot about his plan to leap into the water from the fish. He did not notice the others in the water. Suddenly, he heard his friends calling loudly, "Jump off and come here. The stones are falling from the *pali*."

Makua then saw that the fish had moved away from the land several fathoms. Realizing his danger, he jumped into the sea to swim back to the land. Then the people on land saw a strange sight—the fish opened its mouth and swallowed Makua. A great wail arose, "Makua is dead! The great fish has swallowed him!"

The fish swam straight for the open sea, making the foam fly. When he reached deep water, he dived down and was lost to the sight of the anxious watchers. He swam toward the land of Kane-huna-moku, the hidden land of Kane.

All the people believed, of course, that Makua was dead. They carried this news to his son who was crazed with grief. He ran down to the seashore and hunted on each rocky point for his father's body, thinking that the fish might have eaten only a part of it. On one point he saw an object, but when he had reached it, found it to be only a log. He continued to search until the shadows from the mountains warned him that darkness was near. Then he went home, and falling exhausted by the door, slept until late the following afternoon. At last, a voice awakened him, calling, "Arise, sleeping boy, I can give you good news about your father."

Sitting up, he was very much astonished to see the handsome strangers whom his father had recently entertained. One said, "Arise, fatherless boy. We came to tell you not to grieve. Your father is not dead as the people believe. He has been swallowed by the big fish and has been carried to the beautiful island of deathless people, where he has been thrown up on land, and where he has been received by the inhabitants and where he will be happy."

These words lightened the boy's sadness, but he asked, "When will my father return?"

The stranger replied, "We do not know when, but we have lived in that land and know how fortunate are those who live there. There men never die. So you should rejoice over your father's fate. We cannot say if he will always live there, for we departed before he had had his trials. If he remains steadfast, and does not fail in his trial, and does not violate any of the laws of the land, he shall remain there until the end of the world. But should he fail, you will see him again, for he will be quickly sent away."

The boy asked how far away that wonderful land was, how many days distant from the shore.

The strangers replied, "If the gods permit the land to be moved close to the earth, it takes only an hour to reach it: but if they do not, you may sail the ocean until you are grey-haired, and you will never see it."

When the strangers asked for *awa* and food, the boy prepared it for them and before he placed it before them, he prayed as his father had taught him.

After having finished their meal, the strangers said to the boy, "We are leaving you now, our young friend. Live with hope as you pray to the powerful gods of your father, Kane and Kanaloa. We will care for you so well that you shall not miss your father. No one shall harm you."

Then their bodies began to grow taller and taller until their heads were hidden in the blue sky and their feet slowly disappeared. People passing saw this and thought that the ghosts were returning to frighten the boy, but the boy realized that the strangers were indeed the gods of his father, and he was filled with joy and no longer sorrowed for him.

When Makua had been swallowed by the fish, he had become unconscious. He knew nothing until he was thrown up on land where he was met by two men. Then the gods Kane-huna-moku and Kane-huli-honua came to Makua, and the men went back to comfort his son. His new friends took him to their home, where Makua saw many kinds of fruits and vegetables, bananas, and sugar cane of great size. The taro grew until it had no eyes. He also saw a beautiful, clear lake in which swam many varieties of fish. But he saw no houses and no people and so he asked where they were. The gods told him that the houses were inland and he was not allowed to see anyone until he had been tried. If he did not fail in his trial, then he would live forever and at last pass to another world.

WILLIAM HYDE RICE

Makua was eager to hear the laws of the land, but his guides told him that it was not allowed for them to explain. They had the power to refuse him entrance, and to hide the land from the heaven above and the earth beneath.

Then Makua asked, "Should I break the law of this land through ignorance, would I be punished?"

"No," the men answered, "that wrong will not cling to you, but to the one who did not explain the laws. As we draw near to the houses, others will take charge of you, and they will have the power to explain the laws."

Soon Makua was surprised to see two beautiful houses before him. Two men who looked exactly like his guides came out and greeted him, saying, "You have been allowed to set your foot on our land. You shall have one of these beautiful houses which you see. Everything is for you. You will not have to fish, to build, to work. Only one thing is forbidden here. You must not weep nor wail, no tears must fall from your eyes, you must make no noise of sorrow."

Makua asked why no sorrow should be there. His guides replied, "You have no labor here and so the gods will be angry if you weep. We remember the prayers you made when you lived in the land of death."

Makua realized that he was speaking to gods and he wanted to kneel before them. But before his knees touched the ground, he was told to rise in these words, "You do not need to pray here. You have finished your prayers on earth. Here is only joy. That is the reward of the man who has been faithful on earth. You must first endure your trials. Then if you do not fail, you will be received into the fellowship of the gods."

Then the guides left Makua in charge of the new men. Their bodies began to grow and grow until they reached the sky and they slowly disappeared and Makua heard a voice from above saying, "We shall rejoice to receive you when you have passed your trials."

Makua cried out, "I am in great doubt. What must I do this day? This voice from above has startled me and made me fearful of the trials I must pass through."

One of the gods answered and said, "This day we will tell you all. You will become a god with us, if you pass the trials. If not, then you will become a messenger and will tell to men the beauties of this land."

These words were like a calabash of cool water thrown over Makua. They soothed his agitated feelings and he cried, "I am no longer afraid of the tests. I know my gods have faith in me. I am ready to endure the trials. I have faith that I shall resist all temptations. When you are ready, I am ready."

These words surprised the men and they smiled, saying, "We have not the power to try you. That is given to others. But it will not harm you to be ready at all times. You will not know when you are being tried."

Then they took Makua into a house where he saw many delicious looking foods which he had never seen before. There on the table was a pig still steaming, as if it had just been taken from the oven. Makua asked for the people of the house and was told that he would see them after he had eaten. Gods of the same rank as Kane had prepared this meal, Kane Nee-nee and Kane-Paina.

When Makua had finished his meal, he was taken to a beautiful seat from where he noticed a woman and a boy enter. He again asked for his trial, but was told as before not to be anxious, he would not know when it would be, he should have faith that he would stand fast during his temptation.

The woman and the boy who had entered were still in the background. The woman was none other than the spirit of Makua's wife. The boy was his son whom he had left at home. He had been put to sleep in his house and his spirit had been brought here by the gods. Both wife and son had been told all that they should do in the presence of Makua, who was about to be tried.

Makua heard the woman asking the boy how he had reached this land hidden from mortals, and heard her warning him that he would be killed, if discovered. He heard the boy's reply that he had swum hither because he was told that his father, who had been eaten by a big fish, had been thrown up there.

Listening eagerly, Makua heard the boy say further, "I cannot swim back. I have just escaped death from the cold water. My body became stiff and if I had not been washed ashore, I should have perished."

The woman replied, "Then we must both swim across the great sea so that you can return to life with your father."

The boy answered, "My father is dead. A big fish swallowed him."

His mother urged him to leave with her before he was killed by the guards and she quickly led him out of the house.

Makua asked his guide if he might follow to see what the woman was doing with the boy. The guard told him he might become lost and when the time for his trial, his examiners would grow weary looking for him. But Makua promised not to wander far off. So he followed the woman and boy and soon recognized them as his wife, long since dead, and his son, whom he had left safe at home. Love for them surged up in his heart. Tears came to his eyes, but remembering the law of the land, he refrained from weeping. He thought that the gods had brought his wife to life again, but he feared to speak to her, thinking he might weep, and so he followed far behind them until he came to the beach where the big fish had thrown him upon the sand.

There he saw his wife trying to force the boy into the sea to swim across the water to his home. Noticing that his wife did not show affection for the boy, the father was about to interfere, but he feared he would be recognized. So the boy was forced into the sea, and when he reached the deep water, he cried out, "Oh, Mother, the sharks will eat me." Instantly, he was caught by a shark who swallowed all but his head, and swam off with him. His wife followed the boy into the water and soon Makua saw the big surf roll her over and over, and heard her cry out, "Oh, Makua, my beloved husband, you are watching me die. If I die, you will never see me again."

Makua could endure this agony no longer, and as the waves carried the body of his beloved one up on the sand, he lifted it onto dry land and bathed the face. Tears rolled down his cheeks, but he still refrained from loud cries of sorrow, as he did not want his guides to hear him. Wondering what to do with the body, he was surprised to see that there was still life in it. Slowly, his wife grew strong and throwing her arm about his neck, she wept bitterly. Makua then realized that he had failed in his trial and could not live in this land of the gods, so he led his wife toward the beautiful house.

When they reached the spot where it had been, they were surprised to find that it had vanished. They rested under the branches of a big tree and there fell asleep. Soon a voice calling, "Makua, where are you?" awakened him.

Makua at first could see no one, but he was afraid because he had not been strong enough in the temptation which had come to him. He knew that he must return to earth, and tell his friends there about the beauties of the hidden land and the power of the gods. As Makua looked, he saw that his wife had disappeared and he also saw eight men all exactly alike coming toward him, and he told them how his great love for his wife had made him weep when he saw her in danger.

One of the men said to him, "Hear now the sentence we shall give you. Because you have broken the laws of this land, you must be sent back to the land where men die. When you are very old, death shall befall you. Your body will be destroyed, but your spirit will come to us, though you cannot become a god. Your son will become a god, and he will rescue you from those who keep you in bondage and will rescue your wife's spirit, too. You and your wife will live again through the good deeds of your son."

Suddenly a very dazzling light shone. The eight men disappeared. Makua saw that the heavens were open and he beheld two bodies clothed in light and accompanied by many spirits arrayed in glorious raiment, but with sorrowful countenances. The spirits spoke, saying, "Dust to dust," and then the doors of the heavens closed.

Makua realized that the people of heaven were very sad because he had not been strong enough to resist his weakness.

He hurried into the beautiful wood, where he met the men whom he had seen when he had been thrown upon the sand. They asked where he was going, and Makua replied that he did not know, as there was no one to guide him. They then told him to follow a road which led to the sea where he would find many men and women bathing.

So Makua walked on and he saw that he was on a point of land running out into the sea where people were bathing. As he stood there, he heard a voice calling, "Do not stand on the big fish of your gods. Do you not see that you are standing on the scales of the fish which brought you here?"

Then Makua feared that he would again be swallowed by the fish. The fish seemed like a canoe leaving the beach where it had been tied. As it sped swiftly from the land, the people called aloha. The fish swam toward Koolau, and Makua, overcome with sleep, lay down and fell into a deep sleep. For three days and three nights the fish carried the sleeping man and then safely landed him on the sand at Koolau and waited near until he was found by a man, who thought him to be a ghost, and who ran quickly to tell his friends that he had seen Makua's ghost.

Others hurried to the spot and heard his deep breathing. As they wakened him, he heard them saying, "This is not Makua's body. It is the body of a spirit. We have seen him swallowed by the big fish."

Makua opened his eyes and saw a great crowd curiously watching him. His friends took him to their home and having given him food, asked him to tell all his experiences, and how he had come back from death.

So Makua told all that had happened to him from the moment he

WILLIAM HYDE RICE

had been swallowed by the fish. His friends considered him very foolish to have broken the laws of the land that is hidden from the eyes of man.

Now we shall see what Kane and Kanaloa had been doing. They had put the boy to sleep and had taken his spirit to the hidden land to meet his mother. The boy slept peacefully until the shark bit his body in two. This wakened him, and remembering his dream, he was very sad. But he recalled the words of the gods, and was comforted by the thought that his father was happy in the land of the blest. So he went to the farm, where he again fell asleep and in his dreams saw his father's return and knew all his story. This great joy awakened him, and he was sad to find it only a dream. So he took his carrying stick and returned home with his burden. There he was greatly astonished to see his father sitting before the door and wailing—he ran to him and heard his story.

Makua was now too old to work. The boy labored for him, getting food and fish. In due time the father died and the boy, wrapping the body in tapa, carried it to a cave near Koolaupoko and there Makua was buried.

Glossary

It is the purpose of this glossary to give the meaning of the Hawaiian words used in the text and to serve as a guide to pronunciation. The vowel sounds in Hawaiian—with a few exceptions—are as follows:

a (ah), as in father, alms.
e (eh), as in obey, prey.
i (ee), as in sheet, meet.
o (oh), an in open, bone.
u (oo), as in loot, too, fool.

Although each vowel is generally pronounced separately, the following combinations are sometimes pronounced together in a single syllable:

ai, as i in quiet, or as y in fly.
au, as ow in cow.
ei, as ay in day.
iau, as yow in yowl.
oi as oy in boy.

A-a (a'a').—Rough lava stones.

Akua (a-ku'a).—The name of any supernatural being, the object of fear or worship—a god, a ghost, a demi-god, a spirit.

Aloha (a-lo'-ha).—A word expressing different feelings or emotions such as love, affection, gratitude, kindness, pity, tenderness, compassion, grief; also the common salutation at parting or meeting for greeting or farewell.

Apau (a-pa'u).—Beware.

Auamo (au-a'-mo).—A lifting or carrying stick, like a yoke; a staff or pole for carrying a burden (**au**: a handle, and **amo**: to carry).

Awa (a'-wa).—1. Kava (*Piper methysticum*), a bitter, acrid tasting plant from the root of which an intoxicating drink is made. 2. The liquor expressed from the root of the plant. The drinking of **awa** causes the skin to crack and flake off.

Day of Kau (Kau).—The longest day in the year, Midsummer Day.

Hala (ha'-la).—The **puhala** or screw-pine tree (*Pandanus odoratissimus*) from the dried leaves of which mats are woven.

Puhala really means a group or clump of hala trees. As they usually grow together, **puhala** is the word generally used.

Halemaumau (Ha'le-mau'-mau').—The crater of Kilauea volcano.

Heiau (hei'-a-'u).—A sacred place or temple for the worship of one or more of the Hawaiian gods. (The three principal gods were Ku, god of the land; Lono, god of the sea; and Kane, the supreme god. The large public heiaus were usually enclosed with stone walls. One of the six houses of every chief's regular establishment served as a private heiau. A heiau was sometimes called an unu.)

Hula (hu'la).—1. To dance; to play an instrument and dance; to sing and dance. 2. The dance itself. To be proficient in the art of the hula meant a long and arduous training in the various dances, as well as a knowledge of *mele* and musical instruments. The novice was subject to a number of strict rules as to diet, habits, etc. For instance, a pupil was not allowed to eat sugar cane, as it might spoil the voice, nor to sit on a stone for fear of stiffness. Before being allowed to perform in public, the would-be dancers had to pass a severe examination, after which they received the *uniki*, the secret sign or religious ceremony. Some of the hulas and musical instruments used with them were: the **hula-uli'-uli'**, in which the dancers rattled small double gourds, filled with pebbles, and trimmed with feathers; the **hula-apuwai**, which was accompanied by the beating of hands on double calabashes, which stood from two and a half to three foot high; the **hula-ka-la-au**, in which a long, resounding stick was struck with other sticks, in time. A large drum made from the hollowed trunk of a coconut tree over which a shark's skin was stretched was frequently used. Another dance was the **hula-puili** in which the dancers were seated on the ground, holding in their hands joints of split bamboo, which rattled as the dancers beat with them and passed them from one to another. With all these hulas there was an accompaniment of singing or chanting, called the *oli*, sometimes sung by the dancers themselves and sometimes by others. In learning the art of the **hula**, each pupil had also to learn the art of the *apo*, "catching" or committing to memory, which was to repeat exactly, word for word, after hearing it only once, a *mele*, which sometimes took hours to recite.

Ieie (i'e-i'e).—*Freycinetta arnotti,* a climbing shrub which has a rigid stem about an inch in diameter, numerous climbing and aerial roots, stiff rough leaves from one to three feet long, and a large, handsome leaf-like flower, rose and vermillion in color. Ropes and baskets were made of the woven roots.

Imu (i'mu).—A place or oven for baking meats and vegetables underground by means of heated stones.

Iwi-kua-moo (I'wi-ku'a-mo-o).—Literally, the backbone. The king's chief retainer. This title was the highest honor a king could confer on a subject.

Kahili (ka-hi'-li).—A brush made of feathers tied to a long stick, used as a symbol of royalty. The smaller **kahili** were waved over a king or high chief; the large ones were carried in royal processions. They somewhat resembled large feather dusters.

Kahu (ka'hu).—An attendant on a person of high rank. The relation between the kahu and his chief was very close and permanent, and extended to the whole family of the **kahu**. At the death of a chief a specially favored **kahu**, called *moe-puu*, was killed that his spirit might not be alone on his journey to the next world. To be a *moe-puu* was esteemed a great honor.

Kahuna (ka-hu'-na).—1. A priest, one who offers sacrifice, a physician, an astrologer, a sorcerer, a diviner. 2. A term applied to such persons as are masters of their craft, trade, art, or profession— for example, **kahuna kalaiwaa**, head canoe maker.

Kapu (ka'-pu) or Tapu (ta'-pu).—Eng. tapa, tabu, taboo: 1. A general name of the system of religion that formerly existed in the Hawaiian Islands. The system was based on numerous restrictions or prohibitions, keeping the common people in obedience to the chiefs and priests, though many of the *kapu* included all classes of people. 2. Prohibited, forbidden. 3. To set apart, to prohibit from use, to make sacred or holy, or consecrated.

Kea-pua (ke'a pu'a).—A game in which an arrow made of the shaft of a sugar cane blossom was shot or thrown from a whiplike contrivance.

Kii (k'-i).—An image or images.

Kilu (ki'-lu).—A game in which a gourd was thrown at a particular person, who, if hit, had to sing an *oli*.

Koa (ko'a).—*Acacia koa*, a large hardwood tree growing in the mountains. Canoes and utensils are made from the wood, which takes a high polish and is sometimes called Hawaiian mahogany. The leaf is silvery green and crescent shaped.

Keae (ka-a'e).—*Phaethon rubricauda* or *lepturus* (if white); variously called the tropic, or bo'sun bird. A large white bird with two long, slender red feathers in its tail; in one variety the two feathers are white. It makes its nest in the cliffs.

Koko (ko-ko).—Network of braided strings used for carrying a calabash.

Konane (ko-na'-ne).—A game resembling checkers or chess but more complicated than checkers. It was played with pebbles, or sea-beans, on a marked rock.

Konohiki (ko-no-hi'-ki).—An overseer of the land under the chiefs—the principal man of a village.

Koali, also Kowali.—The convolvulus vine, the morning glory.

Kuina-kapa (ku-i'-na-ka'-pa) Or Kuina-Kapa-Pa'u-pa'u.—A set of sleeping tapas, generally five beaten or fastened together at one edge, answering the purpose of bed coverings. They were very warm. When a favored guest came to a house, he was given a new set, and he was expected to take it with him when he left.

Kukui (ku'-ku-i).—The name of a tree, *Aleurites moluccana,* and also of its nut. The nut, which was very oily, was used to burn for lights or was strung on bamboo for torches. The tree produces a gum. In ancient times the trunks were sometimes made into canoes, but the wood was not very durable; the bark of the root was used in coloring canoes black. The *kukui* is sometimes called the candlenut tree.

Kupua (ku-pu'a).—The demi-god of a locality, beneficent or evil, as the case might be. A localized spirit, often embodied in a rock or a tree or even in a point of land, to be propitiated by specified offerings. A derived meaning signifies a sorcerer.

Lama (la'ma).—*Mabo sandwicensis,* a species of forest tree of very hard wood, used in building houses for the gods. It has a handsome red berry.

Lauae (lau-a'e).—The sweet potato fern (*Polypodium spectrum*). The most fragrant species of this fern grows only on Kauai. Tapa was beaten with **lauae** leaves to scent it (*maile, mokihana,* and sandalwood were also used for this purpose).

Lauhala (lau-ha'-la).—The pandanus or **hala** tree; more properly the leaf of the hala tree, which, when dried, is used for weaving mats and for other purposes.

Laulau.—Bundles of pork wrapped in ti leaves and cooked in an *imu*.

Lehua (le-hu'-a) or Ohia Lehua.—*Metrosideros polymorpha,* a valuable hardwood tree, growing on the uplands of all the islands. It bears a beautiful blossom, generally scarlet, but some trees bear orange, yellow, or white flowers.

Lei (lei).—A wreath or garland: an ornamental headdress or necklace. Leis are made of beads, seeds, nuts, feathers, green leaves, flowers, and other materials.

Leilehua (le'-i-le-hu'a).—A wreath of *lehua* blossoms. (See **lei** and **lehua**.)

Lei palaoa (le'-i-pa-la'o-a).—A necklace, made of many strands of braided human hair, from which depended a carved hooklike ornament of whale or walrus tusk, wood, or human bone, preferably that of an enemy chief. Kualoa lands of Oahu were always reserved by the king for his own use, because dead whales or walrus were likely to come ashore there.

Limu (li'mu).—1. A seaweed. 2. A general name for every kind of edible herb that grows in the sea.

Limu Lipoa (li'-mu li-po'a).—A choice, scented, edible seaweed. It is rose pink in color, and found only at certain seasons.

Luau (lu'au).—1. A feast. (*Paina* is the better word for feast, but **luau** is the modern term.) 2. The young leaf of the *kalo* or taro. 3. Boiled taro leaves.

Luna (lu'-na).—A person who is over others in office or command. Hence an overseer, an officer, a director, a herald or a messenger, one sent on business by a chief, an ambassador, an executive officer of any kind.

Maile (ma'i-le).—*Alyxia olivaeformis,* a vine with fragrant green leaves of which wreaths are made.

Malo (ma'-lo).—A strip of tapa or cloth girded about the loins of men. In former times the **malo** was the only garment worn by men at work.

Malo-pua-kai (ma'-lo-pu'a-ka'i).—Literally, flower of the sea. A red **malo** used for surfing, made waterproof and dyed red by soaking in a mixture of *kamani* oil and crushed *hame* or *haa* berries.

Mamo (ma'-mo).—*Drepanis pacifica,* a species of bird, black with yellow on lower part of back, base of tail and legs. Much valued for cloaks, helmets, and other feather work.

Manu (ma'-nu).—The carved prows of a canoe.

Mele (me'-le).—1. A song; the words or subject of a song, epic in character. 2. To chant or sing.

Menehune (me-ne-hu'-ne).—A race of mythical dwarfs from two to three feet in height, who were possessed of great strength; a race of pygmies who were squat, tremendously strong, powerfully built, and very ugly of face. They were credited with the building of many temples, roads, and other structures. Trades among them were well systematized, every Menehune being restricted to his own particular craft in which he was a master. It was believed that they would work only one night on a construction and if unable to complete the work, it was left undone.

Mo-o (mo'-o).—A huge mythical lizard or monster worm.

Oil (o'-li).—1. A song, a singing; a chant, a chanting. 2. To sing; to chant.

O-o (o-o).—An instrument made of hard wood anciently used in cultivating the ground. It was long and flattened at one end to form a digger.

O-o (o-o).—*Moho nobilis,* a species of bird found formerly in great numbers in Hawaii. The bird has a tuft of yellow feathers under each wing. The yellow feathers were much valued for making cloaks, helmets, and other articles for the chiefs.

Opae (o-pa'e).—The shrimp (*Macrobachlum grandimanus*).

Opihi (o-pi'-hi).—A limpet (*Helcioniscus exaratus*), a species of small shellfish with mottled black, gray and white shell, generally found clinging to moss-grown rocks on the seacoast.

Pali (pa'-li).—A precipice, a high cliff or cliffs, the side of a steep ravine, a steep hill.

Pa-u (pa-u').—A skirt of tapa worn by the women, or dancers—the principal garment of Hawaiian women in former times. It generally consisted of a number of pieces of tapa, usually five, wound around the waist and reaching to about the knee.

Pikoi (pi-koi).—A weapon used in warfare and in robbing or plundering. It was made of a piece of hard wood about two feet long, to which was attached long rope, the other end of which was tied to the wielder's wrist. When the pikol was thrown, the rope entangled the victim.

Pili Grass (pi-li).—*Andropogon contortus,* a long, coarse grass used in thatching houses.

Poi (poi).—A paste-like substance, generally made of the gray root of the *kalo* or taro, but is sometimes made of sweet potato or breadfruit. **Poi** made from taro was the chief food of the Hawaiians.

Poi Board.—A board on which poi was pounded or prepared.

Pola (po'-la).—The high seat or platform between the canoes of a double canoe or a platform built across a single canoe.

Poopaa (poo-pa'a).—(Literally: hard heads) A Hawaiian fish, very easy to catch. Sometimes called *oopu-kai* (*Cirrhitus marmoratus*).

Puhala (pu-ha'-la).—The pandanus; a group of **hala** trees.

Punee Mats (pu' ne'e).—The mats of a **punee** or bed, serving an springs and mattress.

Tapa (ta'-pa) or Kapa.—1. The cloth beaten from the bark of the *wauke*, or paper mulberry, and other similar trees. 2. Clothes in general; a cloak or shawl.

Taro (ta-ro) or Kalo.—*Colocasia antiquorum v. esculentum,* a well-known starchy vegetable of the Hawaiian Islands, of which there are at least thirty-six varieties. It is a species of *Arum esculentum,* cultivated in artificial water beds and also on high, mellow, upland soil. It is commonly made into a food by baking and pounding into a hard paste. After fermenting and slightly souring it is diluted with water, then becoming poi.

Ti or ki.—*Cordyline terminalls,* a plant growing to twelve feet in height with long, shiny green leaves, often used in cooking and in carrying bundles of food; sometimes also for thatching roofs.

Ukiuki (u-ki'-u-ki').—A shrub or plant, braided into a strong rope, often used to bind the thatching of houses.

Ulua (u-lu'-a).—A large Hawaiian fish of the genus Carangus, very much prized for eating. In the dedication of a new heiau an **ulua** was the preferred sacrifice. If one could not be caught, the *mu* (executioner) took the first man he met, for the sacrifice. A hook was placed in the victim's mouth, as if he had been a fish.

Uniki (u-ni'ki).—A secret sign; a religious ceremony for initiation.

Uwau (u-wa'u).—A water fowl.

Wi (wi).—*Neritina granosa,* a freshwater snail or shellfish.

Wiliwili (wi'li-wi'li).—*Erythrina monosperma,* a large tree, the timber of which is, for its buoyancy, made into outriggers for canoes. In former times the best surfboards were also made of **wiliwili**. The tree has a handsome flower, generally scarlet, but more rarely orange, yellow, or white.

A Note About the Author

William Hyde Rice (1846–1924) was a businessman, politician and author. Born in Honolulu, Rice was the only son of two Protestant missionary teachers. Showing an early interest in Hawaiian culture, Rice would begin procuring knowledge of Hawaiian myth and legend, with Hawaiian being his first spoken language. By age twenty-four, Rice had begun to serve the Hawaiian House of Representatives and just two years later would form the Kipu Plantation and Lihue Ranch, ensuring his family's continued wealth and making them one of the top private landowners on the island. In 1887, while working as a senator, Rice would help draw up the Constitution of the Kingdom of Hawaii and be one of the thirteen committeemen who would force King David Kalākaua to sign. Rice would continue to assist the United States in the overthrow of the Hawaiian monarchy and colonization of the islands by betraying Queen Lili'uokalani and placing her under house arrest in 1893; later continuing his political career in the newly formed and short-lived Republic of Hawaii from 1895 to 1898. While his extensive knowledge of Hawaiian culture would lead to the publication of *Hawaiian Legends* (1923) Rice's admiration for the islands would be overshadowed by his act of treachery against Hawaii and her people.

A Note from the Publisher

Spanning many genres, from non-fiction essays to literature classics to children's books and lyric poetry, Mint Edition books showcase the master works of our time in a modern new package. The text is freshly typeset, is clean and easy to read, and features a new note about the author in each volume. Many books also include exclusive new introductory material. Every book boasts a striking new cover, which makes it as appropriate for collecting as it is for gift giving. Mint Edition books are only printed when a reader orders them, so natural resources are not wasted. We're proud that our books are never manufactured in excess and exist only in the exact quantity they need to be read and enjoyed.

Discover more of your favorite classics with Bookfinity™.

- Track your reading with custom book lists.
- Get great book recommendations for your personalized Reader Type.
- Add reviews for your favorite books.
- AND MUCH MORE!

Visit **bookfinity.com** and take the fun Reader Type quiz to get started.

Enjoy our classic and modern companion pairings!

Printed in the USA
CPSIA information can be obtained
at www.ICGtesting.com
JSHW021302231023
50684JS00004B/56